Chronicles of My Life

DONALD KEENE

Chronicles of My Life

AN AMERICAN IN THE HEART OF JAPAN

ILLUSTRATIONS BY AKIRA YAMAGUCHI

COLUMBIA UNIVERSITY PRESS ⊠ NEW YORK

Columbia University Press
Publishers Since 1893
New York   Chichester, West Sussex

Copyright © 2008 Donald Keene

Library of Congress
Cataloging-in-Publication Data
Keene, Donald.
   Chronicles of my life : an American in the heart
of Japan / Donald Keene ; illustrations by Akira
Yamaguchi.
        p. cm.
   ISBN 978--0--231--14440--7 (cloth) —
   ISBN 978--0--231--14441--4 (pbk.) —
   ISBN 978--0--231--51348--7 (electronic)
   1. Keene, Donald.   2. Critics—United States—
Biography.   3. Japanologists—United States—
Biography.   I. Yamaguchi, Akira.   II. Title.
   PL713.K43A3   2008
   895.609—dc22   2007038841
   [B]

Chronicles of My Life

1

When I was a child (and even much later), there was almost nothing to make me think of Japan. The word *kimono* (however I pronounced it) was probably the only word of Japanese I knew, but thanks to my collection of postage stamps, I was aware that Japanese and Chinese writing was similar or perhaps the same. That was the extent of my familiarity with the Japanese language and Japanese culture. I never saw a Japanese film, never listened to a Japanese piece of music, never heard a word of Japanese spoken. It was not until I was in junior high school that I even saw a Japanese, a girl in my class. I knew infinitely less about Japan than the average Japanese boy knows about America.

A Japanese boy is almost certainly familiar with at least the English words relating to baseball. He will have noticed the names of the players written in roman letters on the back of their uniforms and the name of their team embroidered in English on their chests. He will have seen American films, sung or played American tunes, learned the names of a few American presidents and rock musicians. He will know many English words even without realizing that they are foreign.

Although I attended a high school that has produced a surprisingly large number of Nobel Prize winners, our education was more or less restricted to the history, literature, and science of the West. I don't recall a single thing I was taught about Japan in my history classes, though probably Commodore Matthew Perry's great achievement in "opening Japan" was mentioned at some point. When I was about ten, I received at Christmas an encyclopedia for children that had three supplementary volumes, one each devoted to Japan, France, and Holland. I don't know why these countries had been selected. Perhaps it was because they lent themselves to attractive illustrations: humpbacked bridges for Japan, lords and ladies dancing on the bridge at Avignon for France, and wooden shoes for Holland. I also learned from the Japan volume that the Japanese wrote very short poems called *haiku*. That was my introduction to Japanese literature.

Ignorance of Japan was not unusual for a boy growing up seventy years ago in America, but growing up in New York set me apart from other American boys in many other ways as well. For example, Japanese friends, who assume that every American learns as a child how to drive a car, are surprised when they discover that I am unable to drive. Boys who grow up elsewhere in America need to know how to drive, but New Yorkers find travel by subway or bus the normal way of getting around, and relatively few own a car.

I grew up in a middle-class suburb where some people did have cars. My father in fact owned cars of various kinds, the size and condition depending on his financial situation, but they held no allure for me. I preferred the subway and was proud (at the age of nine) to be allowed to travel alone. Cars were not an important part of my life. There were never many vehicles on the street where I lived, and children played in the middle of the street, resenting every car that intruded.

Cars were not the only vehicles. Every morning the milk was delivered from a cart pulled by a horse. The horse knew exactly at which houses to stop and gave the milkman just the proper amount of time to place the milk bottles by each kitchen door. Junkmen sometimes passed along the street in horse carts singing a ditty urging people to sell their used clothes.

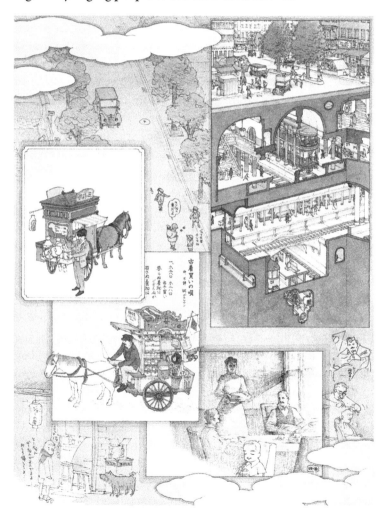

Not long ago, for the first time in more than sixty years, I visited the street where I grew up. I thought then how lucky I was to have lived in a house on a street with trees on both sides, but as a boy I did not realize my luck and wished that I lived somewhere else, anywhere else.

My greatest pleasure was going to the movies. I went cheerfully to the dentist and even to the barbershop (which I hated even more than the dentist) if, as a reward, my mother promised to take me to a movie afterward. I liked every film, indiscriminately, but I was attracted especially to those that showed typical American families living in small towns. The father in the film was always kindly, with gray hair and moustache, and the mother was constantly baking pies. The problems of the boys in the films—whether or not they would be chosen for the baseball team or whether their date would show up on Saturday night—were not problems that bothered me. I envied them because their lives seemed so much more cheerful than mine.

The Great Depression began when I was seven. From then on, conversation at the dinner table often was related to my father's financial problems, a subject never discussed by people in the films. Not much that happened at the time arouses nostalgia. In 1934 my sister died, leaving me an only child. From that time on, the relations between my parents deteriorated in a way that even I could sense. One day my father stormed out of the house, saying he would not return. My mother asked me to beg him to come back. My father asked, "Did your mother tell you to do this?" I said no, and he yielded, but the nightly disputes grew ever more audible. One night I overheard my father say that the only reason why he had continued to live with my mother was that he had loved my sister, but now that she was dead this reason no longer existed. Perhaps he did not really mean these words. They may have been spoken in a flash of anger, but I never forgot them. The final separation of my parents and the move of my mother and myself from our house to a dreary apartment occurred when I was fifteen.

An even more painful factor in my unhappiness was caused by my being clumsy in sports. Unlike the boys in the films, sports gave me no pleasure. I halfheartedly attempted to join other boys playing baseball, but once they discovered how badly I batted and ran, they did not want me on their team. My mother sometimes bribed the boys to include me in their games, but this never lasted for long.

I resigned myself to being a failure. My hope was that when I became an adult (I imagined this would be when I was eighteen), nobody would expect me to throw or hit a ball. Other boys who were poor at sports overcame their inferiority by sheer determination, but I never really tried, sure that nothing would ever improve my ability.

Friends of mine from junior high school days, most of them not seen since then, have written me expressing surprise at what I have published about my childhood. Because their recollections of the past are happy, they wonder why I was sad. Probably I have unconsciously exaggerated my loneliness as a child, and I do have some happy memories, especially of collecting stamps. My friends were classmates who also collected stamps. I dreamed of escaping to a country whose stamps I particularly liked, and I settled on the island of Réunion in the Indian Ocean.

My happiest memory by far was of the trip I took with my father to Europe when I was nine. He traveled to Europe every year on business, and I often saw him off or welcomed him back when he came down the gangplank on his return to New York. Although I repeatedly begged him to take me with him to Europe, he always refused. His reasons were that his trip would take place during the school year or I was too young to understand Europe or he simply did not have the money.

When he mentioned in 1931 that he planned to go to Europe that summer, I saw my chance. School was not in session during the summer. I was sure I knew a great deal about Europe; I had all but memorized *A Child's History of the World.* Finally, I said that if my father was short of money, I knew that a savings account had been created in my name when I was born, and he could use the money for my travel expenses.

That still did not persuade him, so I did something my father had never seen before. I wept for about three hours. Children weep when they hurt themselves or when they do not get what they want, but even as an infant I never cried. My father capitulated. Weeping was the best thing I ever did. We left for Europe that July.

My father and I sailed for Europe in July 1931. The ship was the *George Washington* of the United States Line. It was by no means one of the grandest passenger liners that crossed the Atlantic, but for me it was a whole new world. For one thing, it was exciting to be among strangers and to be introduced to them by my father. In recent years I have traveled several times aboard cruise ships and enjoyed the experience, but my memories of the *George Washington* are totally different. On this ship, my fellow passengers were not rich, elderly people less interested in the destinations than in life aboard ship. Instead, they were of every age and occupation and, no matter how urgent the business that took them to Europe, had no choice but to accept the necessity of spending a week or more on the sea. Ships were the only means to get to Europe.

Of course, the passengers also hoped to enjoy the voyage. The baggage they brought aboard was many times the bulk that is normal today in air travel. The women, especially, provided themselves with different costumes for each meal or social occasion while aboard ship. Even I had my steamer trunk, a heavy metal object that I could not carry or even budge. It accommodated not only my clothes but everything else I might need. My father had used this trunk on earlier travels, and labels were pasted on it with the names of expensive hotels in many cities of Europe.

The ship had no air conditioning. Passengers in first class had outside cabins with portholes that admitted ocean breezes, but the third-class cabins were sweltering, as I discovered in later years when I traveled on my own. Indeed, the dinner table conversations of the third-class passengers often were devoted to argu-

ments as to whose cabin was the hottest, each person insisting that no cabin could possibly be hotter than his own. I went first class this time, thanks to my father who, despite his difficult financial situation, could not imagine going in the steerage.

Much of the day aboard ship was spent stretched out in deck chairs. If the weather was chilly, a steward brought blankets and tucked the passengers in, and from time to time, he brought bouillon or tea. The passengers amused themselves during the day by playing shuffleboard, an uninteresting game that was given some spice by the prizes that the ship awarded to the best players. Ping-Pong was another diversion. My father, an accomplished Ping-Pong player, was the ship's champion that year. He sometimes boasted that on a previous voyage he had beaten the celebrated English tennis player, Fred Perry, at Ping-Pong.

The first-class menu was elaborate, with many choices of dishes for each meal, and as soon as the ship left U.S. territorial waters, it no longer was necessary to obey the American law against serving alcohol. Instead, liquor was ostentatiously consumed. We never had liquor of any kind in our house during the days of Prohibition. Although I knew the location of a speakeasy not far from our house and had seen drunken men emerging, I naturally had never thought of going in. My first taste of liquor was thus aboard ship when my father allowed me to drink the foam on his beer.

The one unpleasant aspect of the voyage was the presence of some American boys who were about my age. The first thing they wanted to know was which position I played in baseball. I could not very well tell the truth, that I was no good at any position, so I had to pretend. Without thinking much, I said I was a catcher and from then on dreaded the possibility of having to demonstrate my skill. In the effort to establish a relationship with these new acquaintances, I joined them in their furtive smoking of cigarettes in a corner of the ship where we were unlikely to be observed. For six months after this I stole cigarettes from my father and smoked covertly, largely as a gesture of incipient maturity. I continued to smoke until one day I realized that it gave me no pleasure and I never smoked again.

The first port of call was Cobh in Ireland. Having learned in school that Ireland was known as the "Emerald Isle," I was pleased to see that the hills really looked green. Although we didn't go ashore, someone got me a newspaper. I remember an advertisement on the front page, something like "Try our coffee. Our tea also is good." This made me laugh, thinking that in America a similar advertisement would boast that its coffee or tea was the best in the world. The words "also is good" seemed particularly funny, my first awareness of difference in cultures.

The ship called next at Cherbourg in France, where we disembarked. It was exciting to be surrounded by people speaking French. My mother had learned French in school and still remembered it well enough to compose little poems, but I hardly knew a word. We traveled by train from Cherbourg to Paris. Each station we passed not only intrigued me but renewed my excitement over being, as I had long dreamed, in a foreign country. The name of one station has stuck in my mind: Limolay-Litteray. The cadences of the name seemed very much like the sound the train made as it speeded toward Paris, but I have never found this place-name on a map. Did I only dream this?

I decided on the basis of this first experience that French trains were much better than American trains. I liked the compartments into which the French train was divided, offering a feeling of privacy. In later years, after learning French, I could understand what people in the same compartment were saying, and this added interest to my journey. I also liked the metal tag under the window, urging passengers to open the windows *vivement mais sans brutalité* (in a vigorous but not brutal manner), a good motto to observe in life.

I still have the diary (the only one I have ever kept) in which I described my impressions of France. Reading it now, it surprises me what a prosaic child I was. For example, I say nothing about the hotel where my father and I stayed in Paris except to note with shock that the hotel restaurant charged eight francs (about thirty cents) for one egg. Again, when I recorded my visit to Fontainebleau, I gave the exact number of windows in the palace and noted that a royal bed was big enough for eight people to sleep in it. Perhaps my father was right in thinking I was not yet ready to appreciate Europe.

In another way, however, the trip to Europe occurred at exactly the right time for my education. Like most boys in my class at school, I wondered why we had to study foreign languages. One could travel three thousand miles, all the way to the Pacific Ocean, and speak English everywhere. But in France I became aware for the first time that I would have to learn foreign languages. Although I did not record it in my diary, I remember exactly when I had this revelation. I was seated in the back of a car with a French girl of about my age, the daughter of one of my father's business associates. She spoke no English; I spoke no French. So in a desperate attempt to communicate with her, I sang the one French song I knew, "Frère Jacques."

Ever since then I have felt strongly attracted to foreign languages. Japanese often ask me how many I know, and it is extremely difficult to answer. I have studied to varying degrees perhaps eight or nine languages, but I have totally forgotten some and others I can understand but not speak or can read but not write. Yet even in the case of a language like classical Greek, which I have almost totally forgotten, I am happy that I have had the experience of reading Homer and the Greek tragedies in the original. But I sometimes think that if, as the result of an accident, I were to lose my knowledge of Japanese, there would not be much left for me. Japanese, which at first had no connection with my ancestors, my literary tastes, or my awareness of myself as a person, has become the central element of my life.

In 1931, the year I first visited Paris, a great international exposition was held. The peoples and products of France's many colonies, their names familiar to me from postage stamps, were on display. I had never before attended an exposition, and I went from pavilion to pavilion feeling as excited as if I were really traveling through Africa all the way to Southeast Asia. My most vivid experience is of lunch in the Indo-Chinese pavilion. I was served a fish with its head on. This was the first time I had ever

seen a whole fish on a plate. The eyes terrified me. When I refused to eat it, the waiter removed the plate, cut off the fish's
head, and served it again. But I still remembered the glaring
eyes, and I could not eat the fish, even without its head.

This minor experience demonstrated that for all my fascina-
tion with foreign countries, I was still bound by native prejudices. In the years since then, I have overcome most of my
prejudices with respect to food and now can eat almost anything. Japanese, even taxi drivers who clearly have no intention
of inviting me to dinner, often start a conversation by asking
what Japanese food I dislike. (Nobody ever asks what Japanese
food I like.) They are particularly eager to know whether I can
eat *sashimi* (raw fish). When I say that I am fond of *sashimi*, they
seem disappointed, but they persist, asking next about *natto*
(fermented soybeans), and if I say I eat *natto*, they ask in desper-
ation if I eat *shiokara* (salted fish guts). Of course, I like some
dishes better than others, but I would not find it a hardship to
eat Japanese food exclusively, provided it was well prepared.

But some prejudices remain. I would not willingly eat dog
meat or the celebrated Chinese specialty, monkey brains. If an
Arab host offered me the eye of a sheep, said to be the most delicious part of the animal, I don't think I would touch it, even at
the risk of offending my host. I do not wish to have a glass of
terrapin blood, even though the owner of my favorite Japanese
restaurant insists that it is delicious.

I am surprised now by how much more vivid my memory is of
the fish in the Indochinese restaurant than of the sights of Paris.
All I remember of the train journey from Paris to Vienna, our
next destination, is another trivial incident. When the train
pulled into a station somewhere in Switzerland, I asked my father to buy something for me to drink. A woman came to the
train window selling fruit juice and my father bought a container.
I drank it eagerly and then fell into a heavy sleep that lasted until
we reached Vienna. It turned out that I had drunk not fruit juice

but wine. My father often recalled in later years that he had allowed me to sleep with my head in his lap all the way to Vienna.

I remember Vienna not for the grandeur of this magnificent city but for another momentary experience. At some point in our sightseeing we visited a museum where I saw the automobile in which Archduke Franz Ferdinand and his wife had been riding when a Serbian nationalist threw a bomb at them. The archduke's uniform and the white plume in his ceremonial helmet were stained with his blood. I knew from my history book that the assassination of the archduke had been the immediate cause of World War I, and now I saw before my eyes what had led to the deaths of a million men. It stunned me. Even as a child I was an intense pacifist, sure that nothing was worse than war, and the sight of the archduke's uniform crystallized my hatred of bloodshed. I left the museum unable to speak.

After World War II, I visited Austria several times, especially Salzburg, but I never went to Vienna, still haunted by the bloodstains. A few years ago I finally summoned up the courage to visit Vienna. I searched for the museum, not knowing its name, hoping to exorcise the painful memory. On the morning of my last day in the city, I learned quite by chance about a Museum of the Army. I went in and, without asking the way, walked directly to the bombed car and the bloodstained uniform. The exorcism worked. I still hate war but my uneasiness about Vienna has disappeared.

I have another painful memory of my first visit to Vienna. I saw children of my age kneeling at the street corners, their hands joined in prayer, begging for money. In New York I had often seen beggars and long lines of men waiting for free soup, but the sight of begging children brought home the misery of the Depression as never before. When my father gave the guide on the tourist bus a somewhat larger than usual tip, the man burst into tears of gratitude.

From Vienna we traveled to Berlin. My father decided we would go by air. I was tremendously excited, as I had never been in an airplane before. I certainly would be the first in my class and probably in my entire school to have traveled by air. I looked forward to telling everyone about my experience, confident that it would give me a moment of glory, but I was also rather frightened. Travel by air was by no means common at the time, and I wondered whether it was really safe.

By present-day standards, the plane was extremely small, but it seemed big to me. Despite my fears, I gradually began to enjoy looking down from what seemed a great height at the towns and farms over which we flew. I was invited to go to the cockpit, where the pilot explained to me the various dials that indicated altitude, fuel, and so on. As I wrote in the school magazine after

my return, I was thrilled to learn that the plane was flying at ninety miles an hour. This seemed incredibly fast.

The plane landed in Prague in order to permit the passengers to have lunch. I remember nothing about what we ate, but I remember the name of the proprietor (or possibly the name of the restaurant). It was Vlk. A name without a vowel fascinated me and was one more revelation of the mysteries of foreign languages. When the plane landed in Berlin, the pilot said something in German that I did not understand, but he seemed to be apologizing.

I have a similar memory of Japan in 1957 when I flew in a small seaplane from Sakai to Tokushima. When the plane alighted on the Yoshino River, the pilot turned to the six passengers and said somewhat bashfully, "Please excuse my rudeness."

I have few memories of Berlin. It seemed much like Vienna, a sad city. After a few days we went on to Bremen, where we boarded a German ship for New York. A photograph survives of me climbing up the gangplank to the ship. I am wearing a beret in the manner of a French boy. I have no idea how I came to be wearing it, but it may have signified that I had changed somewhat since arriving in Europe.

What had I learned in a month or so? I now had vivid recollections of the historical figures who had simply been names to me. I had seen Napoleon's tomb. I had seen the cottage at Versailles where Marie Antoinette played at being a shepherdess. I had been to the Place de la Concorde where the guide, pointing to the statues symbolizing the great cities of France, told us that the statue of Strasbourg had been draped in black until after the French victory in the Great War. I remembered the story I had read by Alphonse Daudet about the last French lesson in Alsace after the defeat in the Franco-Prussian War.

I now wanted to learn foreign languages, especially French. When we got back to New York, I asked my father to hire a

French tutor for me, but by this time he really had no money and I had to wait until junior high school to begin studying French. My love of France, begun at this time, has persisted through my life, though it now takes second place to Japan in my affection.

When I returned to school in September, I was a figure of importance, for a while anyway, because of the many stories I had to tell of Europe and the airplane.

All through elementary school, junior high school, and high school, I was always the best student in my class. My marks were so good that I skipped several times without any trouble. Although I was pleased to be singled out for promotion in this way, the results were not necessarily to my benefit. This became particularly apparent when I entered college at the age of sixteen, two years younger than my classmates and still a boy among these young adults. In high school I was not only younger but smaller than others in my class. In order to compensate for my inadequacy (particularly evident in sports), I tried to demonstrate my ability in other activities. I became the editor of the school magazine in which I published my short stories and the author of the plays performed at the end of the school year. But even these successes did not make up for my loneliness outside the classroom.

I was lucky, however, that Miss Tannenbaum, a teacher of English literature, decided to take me under her wing. She had the custom of choosing boys of promise and helping them win a Pulitzer scholarship to Columbia. These scholarships had been established by the publisher, who left a sum of money to provide ten scholarships each year to boys who had attended high schools in New York. The scholarships not only paid tuition for four years but also provided modest amounts for living expenses. In order to win one of these scholarships, one had to be among the best students in New York State, as determined by the results of statewide examinations given every year.

Admission to Columbia involved still other examinations that covered both subjects that I had studied in high school and others (such as ancient Greek and Roman history) that were not taught in my high school. With Miss Tannenbaum's encouragement, therefore, I read widely as possible in literature and history.

The crucial subject was mathematics. It was impossible to receive a grade of 100 percent on an English or a French examination—an examiner would always be able to find some fault—but on a mathematics examination in which there was only one right answer, it was possible. Even though I had no special aptitude for algebra, my memory was good, and so I more or less memorized the textbook. In the end, I did better on the examinations than did students who were considered to be geniuses in math.

If I failed to win a scholarship, I could not count on my father to support me through Columbia. The alternative was one of the city universities where tuition was free. So for fear of not being admitted to any university, I applied to a city university, but my heart was set on going to Columbia. As the weeks passed without any news, I became pessimistic, sure that I would never be able go to the university I had chosen. But on June 18, 1938, my sixteenth birthday, I received a letter from Columbia stating that I had been admitted and had won a Pulitzer scholarship. Four years of study were ensured. In a burst of self-confidence, I decided that I would never again accept money from my parents.

That September I entered Columbia College. Miss Tannenbaum had urged me to study nothing while in college except for four languages—French, German, Greek, and Latin—and their literatures. Columbia required unusually few courses, but it was not possible to avoid them altogether, so I had to sacrifice the study of German and Latin. One required course was Humanities, the reading in English translation of the great works of literature from Homer to Goethe. Miss Tannenbaum, who had studied under Mark van Doren, had told me that he was the best teacher at Columbia, and I managed to obtain a place in his class in Humanities.

The reading assignments for the course were most demanding, and there were innumerable short examinations to verify that the students had read and understood the assignments. The class met four times a week, and generally each week we read two or three works of classical literature and philosophy, such as Plato's *Symposium* or Aristotle's *Ethics*. I was shocked to receive only a B on the first examination. My scholastic triumphs in high school evidently did not guarantee good marks at the university.

Professor van Doren was a marvelous teacher. He was a scholar and a poet and above all someone who understood literature and could make us understand it with him. He never used notes for his lectures but seemed to be considering each work for the first time, thinking aloud. He frequently asked questions of the students, not to test their knowledge, but to discover what the work we had read meant to them. Van Doren had little use for commentaries or specialized literary criticism. Rather, the essential thing, he taught us, was to read the texts, think about them, and discover for ourselves why they were ranked as classics. Insofar as I have been a success as a teacher of Japanese literature, it has been because I had a model in Mark van Doren.

At this time there was a movement in American education to return to the original texts of the Western tradition in order to understand the background of the present. The Humanities course was one aspect of this movement. Another university

required its students to learn four European languages well
enough to read the classics in the original languages. Although
Mark van Doren did not go so far, he believed in the paramount
importance of the great books. I still think he was right, though
the emphasis on the great books is sometimes scorned these
days. Even now, if I give a lecture about, say, Chikamatsu's tragedies, I tend to use Aristotle's *Poetics* as a guide in describing
what is universal and what is unique in the Japanese theater.

Most of my classmates lived in the dormitories, but at my
mother's insistence I lived at home. This cut me off from the
social life at the university, and worse, it obliged me to spend
almost three hours on the subway every day. As a child I had
found the subway exciting, but having to commute five days a
week made me hate it. Even though it cost only five cents all
the way from Brooklyn to Columbia, the subway cars were old
and dirty. The seats were made of wicker, generally frayed, and
the lighting was yellow and feeble. But I could not waste the
precious hours I spent in the subway, so I read books, most of
them in small print. When I could not get a seat, I read standing. Although eyesight was better than normal when I entered
the university, after a year of reading on the subway I needed
glasses.

Van Doren was not the only teacher I admired. The teachers
at Columbia were outstanding, and the classes were always
small. I enjoyed studying Greek under Moses Hadas, a learned
but gentle teacher. Greek is a difficult language, but the texts
one reads even in the first year are masterpieces, with nothing
of the childishness of elementary texts in modern languages.

The study of Greek affected me in an important, though neg-
ative, way. On the basis of having studied French and Spanish in
high school, I believed that I could learn any foreign language
without difficulty, but I discovered that others in the class
learned Greek more quickly and retentively than I did. It was a
humbling but necessary experience.

I also discovered in a class in French composition that although I prided myself on my knowledge of French, it was quite another matter to write it in a way that was not only grammatically correct but stylistically pleasing. The teacher of this class, Pierre Clamens, was a marvelous teacher who gave everything to his students. He was rather like another French professor I knew many years later, Jean-Jacques Origas, a scholar of Japanese literature. His knowledge of Japan was extraordinary, but he gave this knowledge to his students rather than publish it in books.

Mark van Doren's class profoundly affected my way of reading and understanding literature, and it also affected me in a totally unpredictable manner. The students were seated alphabetically in this class, which is why my seat was next to that of a Chinese named Lee. As the result of meeting him four days a week before and after class, we became friendly. I had never known a Chinese before. About my only contact with China (or any other part of Asia) was going a few times with my high school classmates to eat Chinese food.

It had never occurred to me to doubt that the great books of the Western tradition we read for the Humanities class constituted the priceless heritage of all humankind. I did not even wonder whether other traditions had also produced great books. However, as Lee and I became close, I asked him about Chinese literature. The first book he recommended that I read was Confucius's *Analects*. Confucius was the one Chinese philosopher whose name I knew, but I had no idea what he taught or why he was famous.

To tell the truth, I found the English translation of the *Analects* extremely tedious. Confucius' responses to his disciples' questions seemed merely a series of platitudes, not at all comparable to Plato's soaring ideas. Although I did not reveal my disillusion to Lee, I took a kind of pleasure in memorizing what I considered were particularly silly sayings about Confucius. I could not believe that anything so prosaic as "The Master would not sit if his mat was not straight" deserved to be called philosophy.

It took considerable time and extensive reading in translations of Chinese literature and philosophy before I freed myself of such childish attitudes. In the meantime, I had begun to study Chinese with Lee. My first lesson took place when we went swimming at a beach not far from New York. Although I enjoyed his company and learned much from him, we did not have many mutual subjects of conversation. He intended to become an engineer, and literature did not have the importance for him that it had for me. Then, one day at the beach I had the sudden inspiration of asking him to teach me some Chinese characters. He first drew in the sand a horizontal line. "This means one," he said. Two and three were similar and easy to remember. With four the writing became more complicated, but that made learning the characters all the more interesting. I especially liked those with many strokes or unusual shapes, just as I had liked stamps that were triangles or had curious surcharges.

We agreed to meet every day for lunch at a Chinese restaurant near Columbia. After eating a meal that almost always consisted of fried rice and egg foo yong, the cheapest food on the menu, he would take out a novel he had purchased in Chinatown and go over a few lines with me. This book was not intended to teach people Chinese, but each character I learned was a precious postage stamp that I pasted in the album of my memory. Lee also bought a brush and a book of calligraphy, and I practiced writing characters. I became fairly accomplished at imitating the characters, but as another Chinese pointed out after examining my calligraphy, I had not written the characters

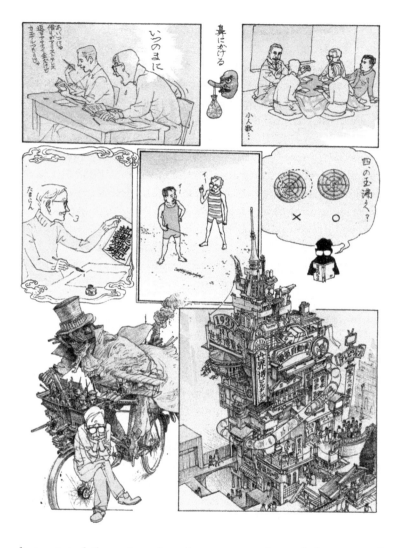

but painted them, ignoring the correct order and direction of the strokes.

Lee and I met five times a week for lunch and a Chinese lesson, but I did not make much progress. Although lessons in Chinese conversation might have been successful, the characters attracted me more. In addition, Lee, who came from Canton, was not confident of his pronunciation of standard Chinese. As a consequence, I learned the meaning of the characters but had no idea how they were pronounced or whether they were in daily use or found only in books. It was not an ideal method of learning a foreign language.

In 1938, the same month I entered college, the Munich Agreement was signed. My friends were outraged at the supine attitude of England and France toward Hitler and the betrayal of Czechoslovakia, but I was secretly happy that war had been averted. Anything was better than war, I thought, and at first it seemed that it had been prevented.

In the summer of 1939 Lee and I went together to the New York World's Fair. We were excited by the exhibits that gave a preview of a brighter world to come. I saw television for the first time and a car that ran on electricity and did not require gasoline. A bright future seemed about to begin, but a month or so later war broke out in Europe.

Ever since I was a child, I had dreaded the coming of war. In high school I had a bright idea of how to prevent the European countries from waging wars: damming the Gulf Stream and in this way making Europe too cold for people to fight wars. But even though I was able to concoct grandiose projects, I could not suppress the fear that if the Nazis were not stopped by military force, they might conquer all of Europe.

At first there was so little fighting between France and Germany that people laughed at the "phony war," but in 1940, the most depressing year of my life, the German army suddenly struck, first at Denmark and Norway and then at Holland and Belgium. The Maginot Line, which was supposed to protect France against German invasions, was easily bypassed by the Germans, and half of France was soon occupied.

Later that year the aerial bombing of Britain began. It seemed almost impossible that the British could resist the

Germans, and I could hardly bear to read the newspapers, dreading the latest news of Nazi conquests. Instead, I spent more and more time trying to memorize Chinese characters, though I realized that this study without aims was an unreal pursuit. But most unexpectedly, in the autumn of 1940, at the worst point of the conflict within me between my hatred of war and my hatred of the Nazis, a kind of deliverance came my way.

At that time there was a bookshop in Times Square that specialized in remainders, and I would look in every time I was in the area. One day I saw a stack of books called *The Tale of Genji*. I had never heard of this work before, but I examined a volume out of curiosity. I could tell from the illustrations that the book must be about Japan. The book, in two volumes, was priced at forty-nine cents. This seemed a bargain, and I bought it.

I soon became engrossed in *The Tale of Genji*. The translation (by Arthur Waley) was magical, evoking a distant and beautiful world. I could not stop reading, sometimes going back to savor the details again. I contrasted the world of *The Tale of Genji* with my own. In the book, antagonism never degenerated into violence, and there were no wars. The hero, Genji, unlike the heroes of European epics, was not described as a man of muscle, capable of lifting a boulder that not ten men could lift, or as a warrior who could single-handedly slay masses of the enemy. Nor, though he had many love affairs, was Genji interested (like Don Juan) merely in adding names to the list of women he had conquered. He knew grief, not because he had failed to seize the government, but because he was a human being and life in this world is inevitably sad.

Until this time I had thought of Japan mainly as a menacing militaristic country. Even though I had been charmed by Hiroshige's prints, Japan was for me not a land of beauty but the invader of China. Lee was vehemently anti-Japanese. When we went to the New York World's Fair, we visited the various for-

eign pavilions, but he absolutely refused to enter the Japanese
pavilion. Although I sympathized with him and his country,
this did not prevent me from enjoying *The Tale of Genji*. No, "enjoy" is not the right word; I turned to it as a refuge from all I
hated in the world around me.

One day in the spring of 1941 I was studying in the East Asian Library at Columbia University when a man I did not know came up to me and said, "I have seen you eating at the Chinese restaurant every day. Would you have dinner with me there tonight?"

Naturally, I was surprised by this invitation. My first reaction was fear that I might not have enough money to pay my share of the bill. But intrigued by the unexpected invitation, I soon agreed. The man, whose name was Jack Kerr, had lived in Japan for several years and had taught English in Taiwan. Although he had some command of spoken Japanese, he had never learned to read the language. One of his students from Taiwan, of Japanese ancestry, had been born in America and had recently returned. Kerr intended to spend the summer at his house in the North Carolina mountains studying Japanese with his former student. He feared, however, that if he were the only one studying, he would not be very diligent. Competition would help, and therefore he was trying to find three or four others who wished to learn Japanese as well. That was why he invited me to dinner.

Despite my love of *The Tale of Genji*, I had not considered studying Japanese because I feared it might hurt the feelings of my friend Lee. But the chance to get out of hot New York in the summer and spend it in the mountains was too tempting to resist.

There were three pupils—Jack Kerr, Paul Blum, and me. I did not know it at the time, but Blum had recently escaped from France. He was considerably older than me—about forty-five to my nineteen—but we easily became friends. He had been born in Yokohama, where his father, a Frenchman, was in business. About the time he graduated from Yale, his father died,

could not imagine myself charging with a bayonet or dropping bombs from an airplane, but I learned of another possibility: the U.S. Navy had a Japanese-language school where it trained men to be translators and interpreters.

Not long after the Japanese attack on Pearl Harbor, I heard a radio commentator declare that only fifty Americans knew Japanese. I wondered whether, on the basis of my summer in the mountains, I was one of the fifty. But the commentator was misinformed. Not fifty but hundreds of thousands of Japanese Americans knew Japanese, and some had been educated in Japan. But the best I could do, with the help of two dictionaries, was to read a simple newspaper article. I could not utter one sentence in Japanese and did not understand it when it was spoken.

I was painfully aware, of course, of these limitations. That is why, when I learned of the Navy Japanese Language School, I wrote to the U.S. Navy Department asking to be admitted. Soon afterward, a letter came from Washington requesting me to appear for an interview. I don't recall what I was asked, but a few weeks later I received a notice stating that I should report to the University of California for induction into the language school.

At that time, a train journey from New York to San Francisco took about four days by the direct route across the middle of the United States. But because I had never traveled in America before, I chose a more circuitous route that took five days. On the day of my departure my mother and several aunts saw me off at the station. My mother wept, perhaps fearing for my safety, but I felt happy. At last I was leaving New York. I did not feel any contradiction between the prospect of joining the navy and my pacifism. I was going to learn Japanese.

My first stop on the train was New Orleans. I had long hoped to see the one American city marked by French culture. Around me on the train were men and women of my age, and soon we began talking, sharing our experiences of travel. I have rarely had a conversation with a stranger aboard an airplane, but when travel was generally by train, it was normal to converse with one's neighbors. People told their troubles and even their secrets to strangers on a train, confident they would never see them again. No matter how tedious a long train journey might be, the atmosphere favored conversation. I wonder whether conversations with strangers on an airplane are so much rarer because one never entirely loses one's fear of flying, thereby inhibiting conversation.

In New Orleans I had time between trains to eat a fine meal at a French restaurant. In the past, I had never been much interested in food. My idea of the supreme delicacy was shrimp in lobster sauce, as served in Cantonese restaurants. But Paul Blum, who took me to various restaurants in New York, had taught me to appreciate the glories of French cuisine.

The next part of the journey took me over the vast emptiness of Texas. I generally enjoy looking out train windows, but for many miles in Texas there is nothing to look at except barren land and an occasional lonely house or cow. Not until the train reached Arizona did I again feel the pleasure of travel. When the train stopped at some small town in Arizona, I got out on the platform and breathed the clean air. It was February, but it felt like a perfect spring day. Why do people live in New York? I asked myself.

The last part of the journey was from Los Angeles to Berkeley, the train arriving late at night. Fortunately, the room I had reserved at the International House had been saved for me. I was very tired and fell asleep, my first night in a bed in five days. In the morning I awoke and looked out to see flowers in bloom and girls wearing sweaters in pastel colors walking along the street. It is probably snowing now in New York, I thought.

Later in the morning I went to the university building mentioned in the letter from the navy. Other men had already assembled. I looked them over, thinking that they would be my classmates, but it did not occur to me that some would also become my friends for life.

We were divided up into classes on the basis of our prior knowledge of Japanese. No class was larger than six. We had classes four hours a day, six days a week, and an examination every Saturday. Two hours each day were devoted to reading, one to conversation, and one to dictation. In addition, we were expected to spend at least four hours preparing for the next day's classes. Although it was not mentioned at the time, we gradually became aware that we would learn nothing about the navy, as it had wisely been decided that this would divert our attention from learning Japanese. We also did not wear uniforms, even after being formally inducted into the service.

Our teachers were mainly *kibei*—Japanese Americans who had been born in the United States, had been sent to Japan for schooling, and then had returned to America. Very few had previous experience teaching Japanese (or any other subject), but they threw themselves into their work with devotion. It did not take long for the students to become fond of the teachers, a feeling that was reciprocated. I did not know until recently that they had been subjected to pressure and abuse from other Japanese Americans, interned in camps in the desert, for their willingness to cooperate with their oppressors. I never noticed the slightest reluctance to teach us; instead, they seemed delighted with our progress in learning Japanese.

The students were divided into two groups. Members of the first had grown up in Japan, the sons of missionaries or businessmen. Some had lived in China rather than Japan, but the navy seems to have considered that this would help them learn Japanese. The other group consisted of people like me who had done well in their studies, particularly in foreign languages. Mostly from major universities on the East Coast, we formed a assemblage of exceptional talent.

For foreigners, the experience of learning Japanese is a major event linking them to everyone else who has studied Japanese. Years later when I traveled in Europe, it was easy to make friends with professors of Japanese wherever I went. Regardless of the country or the differences in our political opinions, the experience of memorizing characters and learning Japanese grammar created important ties between us.

The textbook used at the language school had been prepared years earlier for teaching Japanese to American naval officers in Japan. Unlike the texts I had studied before—some intended for children, others aimed solely at acquiring a reading knowledge of Japanese—these suited the comprehensive method of instruction at the school. We were to be translators and interpreters in a time of war, which required as complete and varied a knowledge of Japanese as possible, and not solely of military matters. For example, someone once came into the translation office at Pearl Harbor with a mysterious Japanese code. I recognized it as notations for *shakuhachi* music, which I had seen at a teacher's house.

We studied hard at the language school, though there was no reward for proficiency. Indeed, everyone who graduated from the school was commissioned, regardless of his marks on the weekly tests. Perhaps there was an element of patriotism in performing one's best in wartime when other young men were dying for their country, but I believe that a more important reason for diligence was the desire of each student to prove that his own university was the best.

After eleven months we graduated. Later groups took up to fifteen months, but we were told that our services were urgently needed. We could now read not only printed Japanese but even some cursive script and also could write a letter or a brief report in Japanese. I gave the valedictorian address, speaking for about half an hour in Japanese, a language in which I could not have uttered one sentence a year earlier.

Most of those who graduated from the Navy Language School in February 1943 were sent to Pearl Harbor. The ship that took us to Hawaii from San Francisco had formerly been a passenger liner but was now old and dirty. It was the worst ship I have ever sailed on, and it was the only time I have been seasick. This voyage made me wonder whether I was meant to be a naval officer. When at last we arrived in Hawaii, it took a week before I could walk on dry land without still feeling the ship's motions.

I was assigned to an office in Pearl Harbor where we translated captured Japanese documents. On our first day at this office we were addressed by a lieutenant of the regular navy who had only contempt for us, obviously resenting that we, who knew nothing about the navy, were allowed to wear the same uniform as himself. (We first wore uniforms after graduating from the language school.) He informed us that the work we were doing was highly secret and that he personally would see to it that anyone who revealed the nature of our work to outsiders would be put to death by hanging.

With these cheerful words echoing in our ears, we set to work translating the documents that were given to us. For the first few days we were excited to think that our secret work was going to help end the war, but the documents were so unmistakably without value that the euphoria did not last long. The documents had been picked up on Guadalcanal, an island in the South Pacific where a long battle had taken place between the Japanese, who had seized the island, and the Americans, who had eventually succeeded in taking it back. By this time the fighting on Guadalcanal had ended and the Japanese there had been killed, but nonetheless we continued translating routine reports on platoons that no longer existed or on the number of sheets of paper and bottles of ink in their possession.

Translating such materials was so tedious that we tried making it more interesting by rendering the Japanese documents into old-fashioned English or into the language of popular fiction. The lieutenant, who knew Japanese, sometimes read over our translations and would then summon us and point out our errors in a rage, translating our English into navy language.

One day I noticed a large wooden box containing captured documents. The documents gave off a faint, unpleasant odor. I was told that the little notebooks were diaries taken from the bodies of dead Japanese soldiers or found floating in the sea. The odor came from the bloodstains. Although I felt squeamish about touching the little books, I carefully selected one that seemed free of bloodstains and began to translate it. At first I had trouble reading the handwriting, but the diary, unlike the printed or mimeographed documents I previously had translated, was at times almost unbearably moving, recording the suffering of a soldier in his last days.

Members of the American armed forces were forbidden to keep diaries, lest they reveal strategic information to whoever found them; but Japanese soldiers and sailors were issued with diaries each New Year and were expected to write down their thoughts. Because they knew they might be required to show their diaries to a superior, to make sure the writer was guided by the approved sentiments, they filled their pages with patriotic slogans as long as they still were in Japan. But when the ship next to the diarist's was sunk by an enemy submarine or when the diarist, somewhere in the South Pacific, was alone and suffering from malaria, there was no element of deceit. He wrote what he really felt.

Sometimes the last page of a Japanese soldier's diary contained a message in English, asking the American who found the diary to return it to his family after the war. I hid such diaries, though it was forbidden, intending to return them to the diarists' families, but my desk was searched and the diaries were confiscated. This was a great disappointment. The first Japanese I ever really knew, then, were the writers of the diaries, though they all were dead by the time I met them.

After working in the translation office for several months, one day I was informed that I was to be sent out on an operation. I would be going with Otis Cary, who had chosen me. Cary, who had grown up and attended elementary school in Otaru where his father was a missionary, spoke Japanese fluently without a trace of a foreign accent, but his knowledge of written Japanese was probably not as good as mine. We made a good team.

We took off from Hawaii in a flying boat, the kind of airplane that had been used before the war for luxurious flights across the Pacific. It had been stripped of its prewar comfort, however, and instead of reclining chairs, we sat on hard metal seats. This was my first experience on a military plane. The plane landed in San Francisco Bay, from where we went on to San Diego. When we reported for duty, we were informed that we would be quartered in a luxurious hotel and that we had no particular duties. There was no indication of where we would be going or when we would leave, but someone dropped a hint to the effect that we should be sure to have an ample supply of white uniforms, worn in hot countries where prewar standards of naval etiquette were maintained.

Cary and I were free to do what we pleased. One day we traveled to Tijuana in Mexico where, for the first and last time in my life, I went to the horse races. And I still have the card of the San Diego Public Library, an indication that I had plenty of time for reading. Even though our stay in San Diego was certainly agreeable, it seemed unreal in the midst of a war. Finally, we received word to proceed to San Pedro and board ship there. The ship was the *Pennsylvania*, a battleship that had been commissioned in 1916 and seen long service. Cary and I were assigned quarters in a tiny room called "The Old Captain's Pantry," which we shared with four other junior officers. Because neither Cary nor I knew anything about the navy until the ship actually sailed, we didn't know which end was front and which back. We also made the mistake of promenading on a stretch of the deck reserved for the captain.

In view of the hint about white uniforms, we assumed that we would be traveling south, but the weather grew steadily colder. But even then we were not told where we were going. Late one night, Cary and I were aroused and told to hurry to the radio room. We made our way in total darkness. The communications officer said, "We've got Jap talk coming over." We listened, but the language was unmistakably Russian. This was the only service we performed aboard ship, but when the war ended the entire crew of the *Pennsylvania*, including us, was decorated because of the ship's outstanding record.

On April 30, at a place aptly called Cold Bay, in Alaska, we transferred from the *Pennsylvania* to a transport. It was pretty clear by this time that we were not bound for the tropics, but only now, aboard the transport, did we learn that we were to participate in a landing on Attu, an island in the Aleutians that the Japanese had occupied. Whereas we still were dressed in summer uniforms, the soldiers aboard the transport were wearing woolens. Although we asked for warmer clothes, we were informed that they had none for naval personnel. This is how it happened that Cary and I, shivering in summer clothes, landed on Attu, where there was snow on the ground.

Aboard the transport we met some nisei army interpreters. They had been told that the navy interpreters were incompetent, but Cary's fluent Japanese changed their minds. Talking with them made me realize for the first time why the navy had founded the Japanese Language School. It was because it did not trust Japanese Americans. It refused to allow even one nisei to join the navy, and therefore it needed non-Japanese interpreters. Even though the nisei in the army demonstrated their loyalty on many occasions, the navy refused them even the chance to die in its service.

9

The attack on Attu was scheduled to begin early in May, but the fog surrounding the island was so dense that the landing was delayed for two weeks. The American ships circled the island, waiting for the fog to lift. Although the Japanese garrison had been alerted to the likelihood of an American attack, when none materialized, they decided that the intelligence reports had been mistaken. That was why the American landing was unopposed.

We left the ship on rope ladders and boarded landing barges bound for the beach. I am not a courageous person, but I felt not the least fear of danger until suddenly I heard a terrible screaming. The ramp of the landing barge ahead of ours had dropped before the barge reached the shore, and the soldiers were thrown into the icy water. This was my first taste of war.

Our barge made it to the beach. Nobody told us what to do once we were ashore, but a soldier said there was a Japanese prisoner on the other side of a nearby stream. We headed in that direction. On the way we saw a dead Japanese soldier, the first dead person I had ever seen. This was a shock, but we continued on, shivering with the cold. The tundra released cold water with each step we took. There was no prisoner.

When I recall now the weeks I spent on Attu, I think first of the cold and the fog. When I had captured documents to translate, my nose kept running all the time, interfering with my writing. Even though we managed to get warmer clothes, the cold was unremitting and it was hard to sleep at night. The landscape of Attu was virtually invisible in the fog. But last year, aboard a Japanese cruise ship, I saw Attu again. The weather was miraculously clear, and I was astonished to discover that Attu is beautiful.

Attu was the site of the first *gyokusai*, called a "banzai charge" by the Americans. On May 28, 1943, the thousand or so remaining Japanese soldiers staged a charge against the Americans, who did not expect such a powerful show of resistance, and came close to dislodging them; but in the end, abandoning hope of success, the Japanese took their own lives en masse, usually by pressing a grenade to their chest. I could not understand why the Japanese soldiers had used their last grenade to kill themselves rather than hurl it at the Americans.

There were only twenty-nine Japanese prisoners. One was from Otaru, and after conducting a brief interrogation, Cary reminisced with the prisoner. Cary seemed extremely happy to have found someone with whom to talk about Otaru, more his real home than any town in America.

We left Attu by ship, assuming that we were headed for San Diego, but when the ship stopped at Adak, a navy intelligence officer came aboard and said he needed us. We had no choice but to go ashore on this dismal island.

During my stay on Adak, I spent about twelve hours a day translating documents captured on Attu. Cary spent much of his time interrogating the prisoners. Although we were within a few feet of each other twenty-four hours a day, we never got on each other's nerves, proof of friendship.

In August the Americans attacked Kiska, the other island captured by the Japanese. For weeks the photo interpreters had said they could detect no movement of the Japanese troops. They believed that the Japanese had left the island, but the pilots insisted that they were still getting antiaircraft fire. The pilots were believed, and the operation went ahead as scheduled. Just before the landing, Cary and I were told that we would land before anyone else in order to ascertain whether the Japanese had indeed left. This seemed like a suicide mission, but luckily for us the pilots were mistaken. There was not a Japanese on the island. But we did find an underground headquarters, and the cushions around the table were made of American flags. On a blackboard someone had written, "You are dancing on foolish order of Roosevelt."

The American troops followed us ashore, and everyone was relieved that there was no enemy to fight. A few days later, however, we had a different kind of shock. The least capable of the navy interpreters came up to me with a sign he had found. He said, "Of course I get the general meaning, but I'm not sure of a few things." The inscription on the sign was perfectly clear: "Gathering point for bubonic plague victims." Messages were hastily sent to San Francisco for plague serum, and for days we looked anxiously at our bodies for telltale spots. Many years later the wife of a Japanese army doctor who had been stationed on Kiska revealed that her husband, guessing the Americans would find it, had written the inscription. It was a joke, but nobody laughed.

From Kiska the navy interpreters were sent back to Hawaii aboard an ammunition ship. Ammunition ships always traveled alone because an explosion onboard would destroy every other ship within miles. To reward the crew for enduring this danger, movies were shown every night. The seats were on sixteen-inch shells in the hold. There were only two films, shown alternatively. I have forgotten one of them, but the other was *Casablanca*, which we saw about fifteen times. In fact, the sailors waiting in line for meals would recite passages from the dialogue to one another. When Hawaii at last appeared on the horizon, I thought I detected its fragrance. In the Aleutians there were no flowers, no trees, nothing but tundra.

During my absence from Pearl Harbor, a new translation office had been established in Honolulu. The personnel consisted of navy officers and army enlisted men, all of them nisei. It was probably because the navy refused to permit nisei, even in army uniform, into the Pearl Harbor base that the office was situated in Honolulu. In order to maintain secrecy, furniture was displayed in a window facing the street with a sign saying the shop was temporarily closed. However, the young women working in the nearby cushion factory or in the restaurant across the street had no trouble guessing that the thirty nisei soldiers must be performing some kind of secret work.

The commanding officer, an army major, was truly disagreeable, but this only caused the rest of us to band together against him. Except when the major summoned us, it was a cheerful place to work. At this office only handwritten Japanese documents—mainly diaries and letters—were translated. Although I doubt that our translations ended the war even one second earlier, reading the diaries was a valuable part of my education as a scholar of Japanese.

We had one day off, which I used to study Japanese literature at the University of Hawaii. The first term we read a modern novel each week and wrote a report in Japanese. The second term I persuaded the professor to read *The Tale of Genji* with us. By this time I had begun to feel confident in my ability to read Japanese, but I was by no means prepared for *The Tale of Genji*. Often I spent an hour or more trying to read just one sentence.

I shared a house in Honolulu with five other navy interpreters. Indeed, I liked living in Honolulu so much that I had no desire to return to New York, but this was not true of my companions, who had wives and children they missed. The pleasant humdrum of work at the office was interrupted from time to time when men were sent out on operations and came back with sunburned faces and stories to tell. Although I hated war, I thought I must experience more of it so that I could understand it better and perhaps write about it.

One day a group of us navy interpreters were summoned to headquarters in Pearl Harbor and informed that soon we would be leaving for Okinawa. The announcement was startling. Up to now the American strategy had been to capture one island after another, but we still were far from Japan. Although it seemed that we would never get there, Okinawa was a part of Japan! The announcement was followed by a doctor's report on the poisonous snakes of Okinawa. We were definitely going to a dangerous place.

I flew from Hawaii to the Philippines, where I was to board ship for Okinawa. Leyte had been the scene of major land and sea battles only a few months earlier, but already a building woven of palm fronds had been erected as an officers' club. But the place had little charm for me, and I soon left it for the Japanese prisoner-of-war stockade.

I hitchhiked to the stockade. The Filipino driver of the truck that picked me up seemed annoyed to learn that any Japanese had survived the fighting, whereas in fact, a large number had surrendered on Leyte. They seemed more disconsolate than the prisoners I had known in Hawaii, perhaps because they had not yet excused themselves for being alive. One of the prisoners may have been the novelist Ōoka Shōhei, who wrote unforgettably about his life as a prisoner.

The fleet that assembled at Leyte is said to have been the biggest in all naval history, consisting of more than thirteen hundred ships of every size. It was undoubtedly very powerful, but it also was vulnerable to attacks by Japanese suicide planes, as we soon discovered. I did not anticipate that the last major battle of World War II would be fought on Okinawa, but I did realize it would be unlike any other battle fought in the Pacific. Furthermore, it would be the first in which a large civilian population would be involved. By chance, my closest friends in the Japanese community in Hawaii were of Okinawan extraction, and I could not put from my mind the thought that many civilians, much like the people I had known in Hawaii, were likely to die in the American invasion.

I had one near encounter with death before the landing. Early one morning I was standing on deck when I noticed in the sky a black point that seemed to be growing larger. After a time I realized that it was a kamikaze plane, obviously heading toward my ship, the largest transport in the convoy. I stared at the plane, unable to move. I would probably have been killed if on its downward path the plane had not struck the top of the mast of the next ship and plunged into the water. A slight miscalculation on the pilot's part had saved my life.

The landing took place on April 1, and much to our surprise, there was virtually no resistance. The Japanese commanding general had decided to abandon the northern half of the island in order to concentrate his forces in the south. There even were civilians on the beach where we landed, including a woman with a baby in her arms and a small child at her side who wandered about aimlessly, seemingly oblivious of the danger. I offered to lead her to a safer place, but she paid no attention. Finally, I picked up the child and carried him to an enclosure intended for casualties. The woman kept saying something over and over that I could not understand, not realizing that many Okinawans, especially women, were unable to speak or understand Japanese.

Later that day, I acquired an interpreter, a boy of nine or ten who had attended school and spoke good Japanese. We went from cave to cave, calling to whoever might be hiding inside.

Some civilians came out, mostly pitiful old people dazed by what was happening around them.

Soon we had our first prisoners, an army lieutenant and a navy ensign. The army officer was quite cheerful, ready to exchange jokes with his captors. After the war I had a letter from him in which he styled himself "Prisoner Number One." The navy officer, much younger, was morose. I guessed that he was ashamed to have been taken alive. He seemed reluctant to respond to simple questions, but a few days later he asked me if I would talk with him as one student to another, not as enemies. I agreed. Thereupon he asked whether there was any reason why he should remain alive. This was not the first time a prisoner had asked me this question. Although I was barely twenty-three and knew little of the world apart from books, I answered the question with confidence, urging the prisoner to stay alive and work for the new Japan.

Many years later I learned that the naval officer was alive and in Tokyo. I sent word indirectly that I would be glad to meet him, but no answer ever came. He may have decided that we would have nothing to talk about. Certainly the bleak stockade surrounded with barbed wire, where we had met thirty years earlier, could not inspire happy memories.

There were many prisoners in Okinawa. A photograph survives of me, sitting on one foot and talking to a prisoner who looks considerably more cheerful than me. I don't know where the picture was taken or what the prisoner told me, but this is proof that for all my cloistered academic career, I once interrogated prisoners in a war-torn field.

When I heard that the Ninety-sixth Infantry Division needed a language officer, I volunteered. For the first time in my life, I had a group of men under my command, ten or so Japanese American interpreters. Initially I was obliged to demonstrate that I really knew Japanese, even though I was a navy officer, but in a short time we became friends. But I never acquired the ability to give orders. If I had to go to a dangerous area, the strongest command of which I was capable was, "Who would like to accompany me to the front?"

The fighting on Okinawa lasted for months. Although I was seldom in real danger, as the summer heat grew more intense, there were smells of rotting cabbages in the fields and rotting corpses everywhere. I had seen the face of war and smelled its odor, which was what I had dreaded since childhood.

I left Okinawa on a ship with about a thousand prisoners, half Japanese soldiers or Okinawan militia, half Korean laborers. Some of the prisoners died on the way to Hawaii and were given Christian burials at sea.

When the ship called at Saipan, a member of the crew made a mistake that admitted seawater into the hold, so we had to wait for repairs. One night at the officers' club a drunken aviator from the neighboring island of Tinian was betting everybody that the war would be over in a month. This seemed absurd to me. I was convinced that the war would last for years, perhaps forever, and that I would die in uniform. Besides, ever since the mistaken testimony of aviators had led to an unnecessary assault on Kiska, I no longer believed what they said. However, this aviator knew a secret that the people of Hiroshima and the rest of the world would know in a few weeks.

Once the ship had been repaired, it headed for Hawaii, arriving in August. I was happy to return to the house that I shared with five other officers, and we exchanged stories of our experiences. That night I had a strange dream, of a newsboy shouting an extra. This was peculiar because there were no such newsboys in Honolulu during the war. But in the morning, when I tuned on the radio, I learned that an atomic bomb had been dropped on Hiroshima.

I went to headquarters at Pearl Harbor to report my return. The commanding officer informed me that I had spent sufficient time overseas to be given a leave at home. He asked, however, whether I would not prefer to go to Japan instead, no doubt assuming that the atomic bomb would cause Japan to surrender. I replied that I would think it over.

I went to the prisoner-of-war camp. The prisoners also had heard about the bomb and some congratulated me, but I was in no mood to gloat. I could imagine how unhappy they must be, realizing that the total defeat of their country was imminent. Gradually they left, probably wanting to be alone, but one prisoner remained. Although we had never talked before, he admitted that unlike many prisoners who felt they could never face the shame of returning to Japan, he was eager to help rebuild Japan and make it a better country. He asked me, as someone who understood the Japanese, to help. I first said no, that the Japanese would have to rebuild their own country, but gradually I yielded to his intensely serious expression. That is how it happened that I left the same night for the western Pacific, expecting I would soon be in Japan.

11

When I arrived in Guam, I expected the war to end at any moment, only to hear that another atomic bomb had been dropped, this one on Nagasaki. I was shocked to hear that President Harry Truman had "jubilantly" announced the dropping of the second bomb. I could think of no justification for this, but a few days later we learned there was to be an important radio broadcast from Japan and guessed it might be an announcement ending the war. Fearing that I might not understand the broadcast, I took three prisoners with me.

The broadcast was difficult to hear. The emperor's voice was faint and there was a lot of static. I caught some words, but not enough to know whether the emperor was ending the war or asking the Japanese people to endure further hardships until final victory. But when I saw the tears in the eyes of the three prisoners, I understood the meaning of what he had said.

A few days later some of the interpreters on Guam received orders sending them to Japan, and before long, letters came from them describing the incredible destruction of Tokyo. The most cheerful fact anyone mentioned in the letters was that the Japanese would barter anything they possessed in exchange for cigarettes. Several interpreters with visions of obtaining treasures began to stock cartons of cigarettes.

I impatiently awaited my turn to be sent to Japan, but this never happened. I was on bad terms with my superior officer. I had always disliked this man, who, perhaps because he was part Japanese, was determined to prove he was 100 percent American and had no sympathy for the Japanese. He hated me especially because I never laughed at his jokes. Now he had the chance to take revenge. He knew how eager I was to go to Japan, so he sent me to China.

This was a disappointment, but I took solace by recalling my Chinese lessons and my first acquaintance with East Asian civilization. I was assigned to the Sixth Marine Division. It was headed for China but needed interpreters of not only Chinese but also Japanese. Although the army had not objected when I wore naval insignia on my uniform in Attu or Okinawa, the Marine Corps insisted that I wear a marine uniform. I felt like a fraud: a short, thin, nearsighted man posing as a marine.

We did not leave Guam until the end of September. The headquarters section of the division boarded a destroyer that reached Qingdao (Tsingtao) before the main body of marines. The night before we arrived, the destroyer was caught in a storm and rocked so badly that I had to cling to the rails at the side of my bunk to avoid being thrown out of bed.

The next morning it had cleared, and from the sea Qingdao looked like a huge picture postcard. I was among the first to go ashore and was instructed to proceed to the International Club. But I couldn't find the club on my map, and while I was trying to remember how to ask directions in Chinese, two Chinese officers approached and asked me in English to guide them to the club. Before long we found the building, a monstrosity of late-nineteenth-century architecture erected before the First World War when the Germans colonized Qingdao. Some American aviators were already living on the second floor. I left my belongings on an empty cot.

I walked out into the street and was immediately surrounded by a crowd of men clamoring, urging me to board their rickshaws. I had never actually seen a rickshaw before, but I thought it typical of the worst aspects of the Western presence in China, as photographs often showed Chinese pulling arrogant foreigners wearing tropical helmets. But not knowing what else to do, I got into a rickshaw and gestured to indicate the man should go straight ahead. Thinking it would make it easier for him, I leaned forward as far as I could. This was actually the least helpful thing I could have done; sitting back would have made it easier. Ashamed that I was using another human being, I dug my nails into the armrests of the rickshaw.

In the meantime, I had become an object of attention to people in the streets. Children, running after my rickshaw, shouted at me; a group of actors dressed in the traditional costumes and false beards of the Chinese theater saluted, as did a work party of Japanese soldiers. Unlike the descriptions I had read of the food shortage in postwar Tokyo, the markets along the streets of Qingdao overflowed with food, cigarettes, articles of clothing, pots and pans. Nobody wanted to barter masterpieces of art in return for cigarettes.

I got down from the rickshaw, gave the man a few American coins, and began to wander aimlessly through the streets. The depression I had felt while in the rickshaw lifted, and I felt exhilarated. I was in China! A Chinese army officer who spoke English joined me and guided me into shops where I bought myself a Chinese robe, Chinese shoes, and a jade ring. "Everything Chinese now but the face," my new friend commented.

The next day I visited the Japanese army headquarters. I did not know how to address the officers because the Japanese in Qingdao had not surrendered. In fact, the Americans soon needed their help in keeping the railway open to the interior. Even though their country had been defeated, they themselves were as prepared for warfare as ever. I saluted and they saluted back.

The Japanese army officers in Qingdao still occupied their old offices, and little seemed to have changed. They treated me not only politely but with friendliness. The war was over, why not be friends? The atmosphere recalled gatherings after a football game when members of both sides happily drink together and remember incidents of the game.

My stay in Qingdao, which had started happily, soured after a few weeks. The streets soon filled with American sailors and with Chinese who sold the sailors articles that were as ugly and vulgar as they could make them. Gradually, too, I became aware of the pervasiveness of corruption in the city. The head of the Anti-Opium League, a professorial-looking man, was a dealer in opium. A Chinese who spoke harshly about the Japanese may have made a fortune during the Japanese occupation. The atmosphere of corruption seemed to be catching: one American officer amassed a collection of art by informing Japanese that if they gave him their works of art, he would see to it that they were safely repatriated. People denounced their friends to the Americans, hoping to curry favor; every morning when I arrived at my office I would see a line of would-be informers.

My worst experience was investigating war crimes. One day, while talking with a Korean, I happened to mention the name of a Japanese naval officer with whom I was friendly. The Korean said with an ironic smile, "Yes, he's a nice man who eats human liver and boasts of it." I asked him in astonishment what he meant, and this led to an investigation of how Chinese, accused of various crimes, had been executed. Without trial, the accused were tied to stakes and used for bayonet practice. It was hoped that this would harden young recruits. Sometimes, I was told, a Japanese soldier cut the liver from the corpses.

I had not been trained in criminal investigation, and the work was distasteful, especially because it involved people I

knew. I asked to be allowed to return to America. I was told
that if I continued my work on war crimes for another month I
would be given a week in Beijing, but I refused. I regret now I
did not see Beijing before the brutal modernization of the
city.

I flew from Qingdao to Shanghai and from there to Tokyo.

The plane from Shanghai flew low enough over Japan for
me to see the landscape clearly. Japan seemed incredibly green
after China, where trees were a rarity. In fact, the trees visible
from an airplane in China were usually those planted around
Japanese shrines. In Japan the villages, not surrounded by
walls, seemed to melt into the forests. Never had two countries
seemed more different.

When the plane landed at Atsugi, I was asked to show my orders. The orders read, "You will return to your original command." I knew that this meant I must return to Hawaii, but I
could not endure the thought of leaving Japan without seeing
the country that had been on my mind every day for four years.
I told myself, "The war is over. Nobody will care if I ignore the
order." So I told the officer that my original command was now
in Yokosuka. He accepted this explanation, and soon I was in a
jeep bound for Tokyo.

The drive to Tokyo was the opposite of normal expectations.
As the jeep approached the center of the city, the buildings grew
fewer and fewer instead of more numerous. Here and there, in
place of houses were storehouses built of concrete or only
smokestacks. Some buildings that seemed to have survived the
bombing were, on closer examination, merely shells. The devastation was even worse than I had imagined.

Not having proper orders, I did not know where to go, but fortunately I recalled from a letter that some language officers were quartered in the Yūraku-chō Building. However, I remembered the name as Yūryaku, the name of a cruel emperor of ancient times about whom I had read in Tsunoda-sensei's class. Although I thought it strange that a section of Tokyo had been named for someone who delighted in shooting innocent people from trees, eventually I found my way to Yūraku-chō. Someone told me that another language officer was now in Nagoya and suggested I use his bed.

It was exciting being in Japan, but what I wanted to do most was not visit museums or the theater or places of scenic beauty, though all of these attracted me. Rather, I wanted to tell the families of the prisoners and the Japanese I had known in China that these men were safe. No doubt the families had been officially informed that my friends had died a hero's death, but I was sure that they would be happy, not ashamed, to learn that their sons or husbands were still alive.

I found the family of my closest Japanese friend in China living in the basement of what must have been a splendid house in Yotsuya that had been destroyed during the bombing. I then went to the Shōnan area in search of the family of a prisoner with whom I had talked many times, not about the war, but about literature and music. Unfortunately, his name was Satō, and even in a relatively small town, there were many people of that name. As I went from one Satō's house to the next, I was followed by a train of small children, but in the end I never found my friend's family.

The only sightseeing I did during my week in Japan was a trip to Nikkō. A phrase from the textbook of Japanese, *Nikkō wo minai uchi wa, kekkō to iu na* (Don't say "wonderful" until you've seen Nikkō), lingered in my memory, and I was happy to accept when several nisei from my old office in Honolulu invited me to accompany them to Nikkō. We naturally went by jeep, American servicemen's favored means of transportation. I had traveled in this uncomfortable but sturdy vehicle across the tundra in the Aleutians and through the forests of the Philippines.

The road to Nikkō was largely deserted, and there were almost no road signs. We had to stop again and again to ask if we were heading in the right direction, and people seemed glad to tell us. By this time, even Japanese living in the country were familiar with jeeps, and when we passed through villages, children lining the road waved their hands and shouted greetings at us and the jeep, apparently delighted we had paid them a visit.

Before leaving for Nikkō we had been urged to take rice with us for our evening meal. We gave the rice to the innkeeper, and that night a miracle occurred. The white rice we had given him had turned into brown, unpolished rice.

When I awoke the next morning, there was snow around my pillow. I walked to the Tōshōgū, the mausoleum of the Tokugawa shoguns. It was completely deserted under a light fall of snow. A boy in middle-school uniform approached and offered to guide me, pointing out the famous sights. "Before the war an American offered a million dollars for the Yōmei Gate," he noted, "but he was refused. Now I suppose the Americans will take it without having to pay."

I have gone back twice to Nikkō, but the first visit was the only one that seemed "wonderful." I suppose I have been affected by more typical Japanese aesthetics, and the lavish decorations of Nikkō no longer please me. Or perhaps Nikkō looked so beautiful in December 1945 because the gaudy colors of the sculptures were softened by the snow and there were no other tourists there.

I spent a total of a week in Japan and did not meet a single Japanese scholar or visit a university. I was told that kabuki was off limits to American military personnel. My contacts with Japanese thus were with people I did not know and would never see again, but they all showed me much kindness. They invited me into their houses and offered me tea and a fragment of a

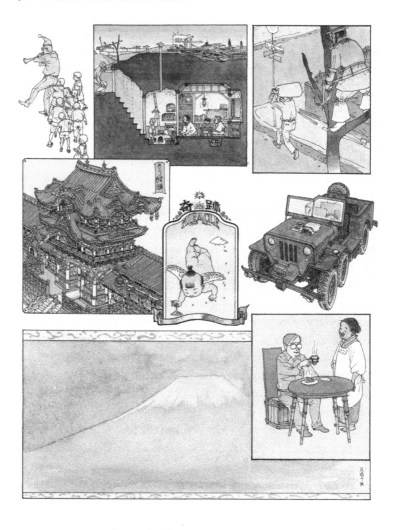

sweet potato in place of cake. I went to a barbershop where I had
my hair cut and was shaved by a young woman. It occurred to
me later that it would have been simple for her to cut the throat
of an enemy officer if she had been so disposed, but I was not in
the slightest afraid. On a station platform I accidentally wit-
nessed the grief-stricken parting of an American soldier and a

Japanese woman. I could detect no trace of enmity of Japanese for Americans or of Americans for Japanese, and yet it had been scarcely four months since a bitter war ended. How was it possible for people's emotions to change so rapidly? I wondered. But perhaps friendship is the normal feeling between peoples, and war is only an aberration.

After a week I began to feel afraid that the navy might be looking for me, so I went to an office in Yokosuka and reported that I had been mistaken, that my original command was still in Honolulu. This was accepted without question. It must have happened fairly frequently that people got lost. I was allotted a place where I might sleep and leave my belongings until I was given a seat on a plane to Hawaii.

The day before I left Yokosuka, I visited a bookshop, looking for some recent publications to take to the prisoners in Hawaii. I overheard two old women talking, one telling the other, "My daughter lived in Yokosuka, not far from the Navy Yard. When the American planes began to bomb Japan, my son-in-law decided it was dangerous in Yokosuka and moved her to Kōfu. Because there weren't any military installations in Kōfu, we thought she would be safe there. But the planes bombed Kōfu almost every night, and Yokosuka wasn't touched."

I remembered asking an aviator why Kōfu was bombed so often. He answered with a laugh that it was easy to find, on the direct route to Tokyo, and there wasn't much antiaircraft fire. It was the safest place to drop bombs.

The next morning I was awakened before dawn and told I was to proceed to Kisarazu on the other side of Tokyo Bay. I hurried to the designated pier, but as usual in the armed forces, this was a case of "hurry up and wait." The ship showed no signs of departing, but at last it moved out in the dark bay. I was standing on the deck, looking out over the bay when suddenly Mount Fuji rose in front of me, pink in the light of the rising sun. This was almost too perfect a departure from Japan. I gazed at the mountain as it gradually changed colors, moved to tears by the sight. Someone had once told me that if one sees Mount Fuji just before leaving Japan, one will return. I hoped this was true, but it would be almost eight years before I saw Japan again.

I returned to Hawaii just before Christmas 1945. I went to the office where I had translated Japanese documents for two years, but the place was deserted, as most of the translators were in Japan. The only people I met in Hawaii who seemed glad to see me were the prisoners. Of course, they had read the newspapers and knew in general what was happening in Japan, but they were eager for details. I tried to answer their questions, but I could not tell them what they wanted most to know, though nobody asked: When they returned to Japan, what kind of reception would they receive?

I formally requested discharge from the navy and asked to return to New York. One day, word came ordering me to report to the aircraft carrier *Saratoga* for transportation to the West Coast of the United States. The *Saratoga*, which was fated to be blown up in the test of the hydrogen bomb at Bikini, was the most agreeable ship I traveled on during my entire naval career.

From San Francisco I took a train to New York. The trip had none of the excitement of my first one across the country. I can recall only the very last stage of the journey, the familiar subway ride to Brooklyn. As I left the subway station, a woman with a boy, seeing the returning hero with his heavy baggage, told him to carry one suitcase, only to decide in the next instant that it was too heavy for him. Such was my return to civilian life.

When I showed my mother the various souvenirs I had brought her—embroidery from China, a Benkei doll in a heroic pose that somebody had given me in Japan—I felt like a tourist returning from his first trip abroad. But when I took out my prize, the sword the Japanese general in Qingdao had given me because (as he wrote) he thought I possessed *Yamato damashii* (the soul of Japan), my mother let out a shriek and said she would not allow anything so terrifying in the house.

Strange to say, although I had eagerly awaited release from the navy, I had never given much thought to what I would do afterward. Most of the other language officers planned to return to their work prior to joining the navy, but I had no profession. I knew Japanese, but this was not much of an asset, as it was commonly assumed that it would take at least fifty years for Japan to regain its prewar importance. Some language officers, deciding that China was likely to replace Japan as the leading power in East Asia, shifted to studying Chinese. But most of those who had learned Japanese lost all interest in using the language. If I met them, they would say with a touch of pride that they had forgotten every word of Japanese, or they would declaim the few phrases they remembered, such as *Teki wo mizugiwa nite gekimetsu subeshi* (Annihilate the enemy at the water's edge!).

As an undergraduate, I had not known what I wanted to become. Every profession seemed equally unappealing, but now the study of Chinese and later Japanese opened up the possibility of an occupation. But what, specifically, was I to do with my Japanese? There was no demand for teachers of Japanese literature or history at any American university.

Although the prospects were poor, I decided to stay with Japanese and trust my luck. People sometimes congratulate me for having realized in 1946 that an economic miracle would take place in Japan twenty-five years later, but at this point I did not foresee this miracle. Instead, I made the choice because of a vague awareness that I was temperamentally suited to studying Japan. Years later, when I applied for a visa at the Japanese consulate general in New York, a young vice-consul said, "You were clever to have studied Japanese. You never would have become famous in anything more competitive." It naturally did not please me to be told this, but he may have been right.

Accordingly, I decided to return to Columbia to study again under Tsunoda-sensei. I was now better prepared than I was four years earlier to read the books he mentioned in class and to understand the quotations he wrote on the blackboard. Four or five other former language officers were eager as well to study Japanese literature with him. Some wanted to read Heian literature, others Buddhist literature, and still others Genroku literature. Because the other teachers of Japanese studies were still serving in Japan, Tsunoda-sensei taught all three periods of literature in addition to his usual course on the history of Japanese thought. We all were eager to work hard after our long absence from the university. In the class devoted to Genroku literature, for example, we read the whole of Saikaku's *Five Women Who Loved Love*, probably the first time any students outside Japan had done so. We also read Bashō's *Narrow Road to Oku* and part of Chikamatsu's *The Battles of Coxinga*.

Tsunoda-sensei was mercilessly exploited, but I believe it cheered him to have young Americans, back from the war, devoting themselves to his country's literature. Japan had been defeated and he felt depressed, but he probably would have been equally depressed if America had lost the war. Although he had no sympathy for Japanese militarism and had decided to remain in America rather than be repatriated, he could not forget the country where he was born. His was the tragedy that anyone who loves two countries may experience.

My graduate study under Tsunoda-sensei was not only enjoyable but provided me with the themes of my future work. I wrote my M.A. thesis on Honda Toshiaki, an independent thinker of the late Tokugawa period who interested Sensei and therefore also interested me. My Ph.D. dissertation was on *The Battles of Coxinga*, which I had read under Sensei's guidance. In later years I translated *Essays in Idleness*, a work we had read in the class devoted to Buddhist literature.

Although I was happy in my studies, I badly wanted to go to Japan. But this was not possible, as the Occupation policy was to admit only businessmen and missionaries. I therefore visited various companies in New York that did business with Japan, only to be told that American companies thought of interpretation as manual labor and paid for it accordingly. It was far cheaper to employ a Japanese on the scene than to hire someone like myself. For a time I thought of becoming an interpreter at the war crimes trials, but remembering my experiences in Qingdao, at the last moment I refused an offer from the government.

I therefore decided that if I could not go to Japan, I would go to China. I took lessons in Chinese conversation for about six months and became fairly fluent. However, a student in my class whose father was a missionary in Nanjing repeatedly reported what he had written about the disturbed conditions in China that made study impossible. Persuaded by her advice, I gave up my plan. Despite all my classmate had told me, she went to Beijing, where she was denounced as a spy. For months she was chained to a wall in a prison cell and every day expected to be executed.

Having given up China, I thought next of Harvard. It was the oldest and richest university in America and its faculty was extremely distinguished. At the language school I had made close friends with some Harvard graduates and thought I would like to study alongside them in unfamiliar surroundings. But how could I tell Tsunoda-sensei I was going to study under another teacher? Although I feared he might be upset, I finally told him of my plan. He answered that it was common for Buddhist scholars to travel from one center of learning to another. The name for this, he said, was *henzan*.

With Tsunoda-sensei's blessings, I went to Harvard in the autumn of 1947. I especially looked forward to studying with Serge Elisséeff, a legendary figure beloved by Harvard students. He had studied Japanese in St. Petersburg and Berlin and then in Tokyo after the Russo-Japanese War. He was without doubt the best-known scholar of Japan in America.

The year I spent at Harvard (1947/1948) was a mixture of pleasure and disappointment. The greatest pleasure was the company of my friend from Japanese Language School days, Joseph Levenson. He had shifted his interest from Japanese to Chinese and before long would publish a series of brilliant works on recent Chinese history. He was one of the most delightful people I have known, a man of great wit and intelligence but utterly without malice. Under his spell I said things and eventually wrote things that had never occurred to me before.

We ate lunch together five days a week. Sometimes we were joined by Edwin Reischauer, then an assistant professor of Japanese history. He never made us feel that he knew more about Japan than we did; on the contrary, he was extraordinarily youthful, almost boyish in his manner. He had not yet published his most impressive work, his great study of the diary of Ennin. The translation of this difficult text, written in a mixture of ninth-century classical and colloquial Chinese, is a model of scholarship and is augmented by sixteen hundred footnotes, each no doubt the product of hours of research.

I was impressed that Reischauer also published a second volume on Ennin that was intended for "those with a more general interest in the broad record of human history." This was not a common attitude among professors at the time. Even Reischauer had previously followed the current fashion of indicating which words, not in the original text, had been supplied by the translator. This meant that such words as *the* and *is* were put in square brackets, making the translation tedious. I doubt that anyone ever benefited by such scrupulous attention to the differences between Japanese and English. Nonetheless, Reischauer's decision to write for the general public prefigured his later educational activities, such as organizing a television series of Japanese films. This aspect of Reischauer's work encouraged me when I began to publish my own books.

Another pleasure at Harvard that year was the course on the poetry of Du Fu (Tu Fu), given by William Hung. In some ways, Hung's scholarship was old-fashioned, but he not only was completely familiar with Du Fu's poems but also had consulted English, German, and Japanese translations to discover what fresh insights had been provided by non-Chinese scholars. My most vivid memory of his teaching is of the time when he recited by heart one of Du Fu's long poems. He recited the poem in the Fukien dialect, his own, which preserves the final consonants lost today in standard Chinese. As Hung recited, leaning back, tears filled his eyes. That is the kind of professor I want to become, I thought.

My disappointment at Harvard was with Professor Elisséeff. He read his lectures from a manuscript that probably had been prepared years before. Although he spoke beautiful Japanese and was fluent in French and German and, of course, his native Russian, his English was poor, and his students (including me) made fun of his mispronunciations and grammatical errors. But the main cause of my disappointment was his sterile presentation. In his survey course on Japanese literature, when he was discussing, for example, an anthology of poetry, he would state the number of poems, the number of chapters devoted to spring poems, the number to summer poems, and so on. This would be followed by his reading aloud a list of the oldest manuscripts, the oldest woodblock editions, and the names of essays by Japanese critics who had discussed the anthology. He never expressed any opinion about the anthology's literary worth or suggested what it had contributed to the history of Japanese literature. An hour might go by without his saying anything I wanted to remember.

Elisséeff also gave me private lessons in reading *The Battles of Coxinga*, which I was then translating as part of my doctoral dissertation. Relying on his exceptional knowledge of Japanese, he probably did not prepare the lessons in advance. So when we came to a passage that he could not understand, he often favored me with an anecdote about Old Russia, before the Revolution.

What disturbed me most was Elisséeff's attitude toward Japanese scholars. Although he probably thought of the Japanese as charming friends, he seemed convinced that scholarship had been invented in Europe and was carried on in America by Europeans. Once, in some connection, I mentioned the name of Tsunoda-sensei. Elisséeff immediately retorted, "How can a university have such a man?" I was furious but controlled my inclination to say, "He knows ten times as much as you about Japanese literature."

In this way, Elisséeff influenced me when I began to teach at Columbia, as I did the opposite of everything that he had done. I carried nothing in my hands when I went into the classroom where I taught my survey of Japanese literature. Of course, I prepared my lectures, but I wanted them to be new each year. I did not state the number of poems in an anthology, but if the students wanted to know this, I would tell them where to look. Instead, I felt that the most important thing I could do as a teacher was to pass on my enthusiasms, my love of Japanese literature, not to relay facts that could easily be found in books. A lecture, I decided, was not the best way to transmit information.

My attitude owed most to Mark van Doren, who had lectured in a way that I considered ideal. I was indebted also to Tsunoda-sensei, of course, and to William Hung too. My goal of writing for the general public probably reflected Reischauer's. And I owed much to Elisséeff for providing a model of what I should not do.

About halfway through the school year, I discovered that I would soon lose the educational benefits provided by the "GI Bill of Rights," which ensured three years of free university tuition to ex-servicemen. I decided to look for a teaching job, but the only opening I heard about, at a small college in Maine, was to teach the history of all civilizations. I did not feel up to this task. When I consulted a professor at Columbia who always seemed interested in my career, he examined my undergraduate record and suggested I might find a job teaching Greek. This suggestion was not welcome. I hadn't look at a Greek book for seven years, and I had no intention of abandoning Japanese.

At this point someone told me about the Henry Fellowships, awarded to Americans for study in England and to Englishmen for study in America. Preference was given to applicants who wished to study subjects that were not as well taught in their own country as in the host country. I thought it would be mistake to apply to study Japanese in England, so I proposed Arabic and Persian. I reasoned that long-standing British relations with the countries of the Middle East had probably fostered the study of their languages. I wrote the usual kind of proposal, stating that persons whose knowledge of Asia extended from Japan to Arabia were very scarce and hinting that I would have no trouble in learning two more languages, however difficult.

To my surprise, I won a fellowship to Cambridge. If I had been encouraged to study Arabic and Persian, I am sure that is what I would have done, but when I told a professor of oriental languages that I intended to learn Arabic during the year of my fellowship, he looked surprised. And when I added that I would also learn Persian during the same year, he suggested that I not bother the professors. I was not heartbroken. I looked forward to a year at Cambridge during which I could study anything I pleased.

When the college servant showed me to my two rooms, he said, "Coldest rooms in Cambridge, sir." I would remember these words as autumn turned into winter. There was no way to heat the bedroom, and the window could not be completely shut. The sitting room had a gas stove that produced a feeble heat detectable only in immediate proximity.

That first day I was given a small jug with about an inch of milk in it, the daily ration, for use in my tea. Meals were served

in "hall," the college refectory. It was a rather gloomy building, the walls decorated with portraits of men who hundreds of years ago had in some way benefited the college. Sitting at long wooden tables, the undergraduates ate very rapidly, manipulating their knife and fork in both hands with a speed that dazzled an American. When they had finished the meal, they unceremoniously left their seat, if necessary stepping on the table to get out. I noticed that they ate everything on their plates. I was accustomed to leaving a little, but when I realized that for young men who had grown up in wartime, food was too precious to waste, I began to eat everything, a practice I have kept to this day.

The food was terrible, in large part the result of the rationing. The entire weekly meat ration was about the size of a one's hand. Although fish was not rationed, virtually the only fish that was served was herring. I once noted that of the twenty-one meals I ate that week, fourteen had herring as the main component. The least welcome dish was whale meat. One could smell it as soon as one entered hall, and the chefs did not conceal its repulsive blackness. But the menu gave fancy French names to everything we consumed, regardless of the taste.

Another feature of life in Cambridge was the importance of the bicycle. Everyone had one; indeed, life without a bicycle was almost unthinkable. Fortunately, I had learned to ride when I was a boy, but it took time for me to learn to use the handlebars rather than the pedals as brakes. Bicycles were everywhere, and some naturally got lost or were even stolen. A brilliant British lawyer once successfully defended a student accused of stealing a bicycle by establishing the truth that a bicycle is a wild animal and therefore does not belong to anyone.

Although I had received a Master of Arts from Columbia, Cambridge did not recognize degrees from other universities, so I was classed as a first-year undergraduate. This did not bother me, but it was the first time in my life I was the oldest member of any group. The students were unlike those I had known in America. They were politically conservative and made many sarcastic remarks about the Labour government then in power. They dressed with care, and their speech revealed that they were gentlemen. (An undergraduate who spoke with a regional accent was urged to take lessons in proper English.) At first I feared I might not be able to make friends with such superior young men, but I was mistaken. Despite their somewhat affected manner of speech, they were friendly and helpful when I needed them most.

The most exciting event of my first year in Europe did not take place in Cambridge. I was informed before Christmas that during the vacation, I would have to vacate my rooms so that candidates taking examinations for scholarships could use them. Just at this time some Americans with whom I had become friendly on the ship across the Atlantic wrote me from Rome, suggesting I spend Christmas with them. This seemed an ideal arrangement. I had virtually finished writing my doctoral dissertation, and there was no reason I could not type it in Rome. I left for Italy with the manuscript and a typewriter. After spending a day or two in Paris, I took the night train for Milan. The compartment was stuffy with tobacco smoke. When the train reached Milan I asked a man in the compartment if he would look after my belongings while I got a breath of fresh air. He agreed, and I walked up and down the platform for about ten minutes. When I got back to the compartment, there was no man, no suitcase, no typewriter.

I went to the police and reported in my inadequate Italian what had happened. They did not seem eager to search for the thief, probably thinking that a stupid foreigner who trusted a stranger deserved to lose his belongings. I never recovered my manuscript, the sole copy. I spent a week in Rome, then returned to Cambridge to start writing the dissertation again.

I told one of my friends, who, because he was the son of a professor, had remained in Cambridge during the vacation, what had happened. Soon after, I heard from his mother, Mrs. Dickins. Realizing what a shock I had undergone, she invited me to have lunch every day at her house until the new term began. Another friend arranged for me to have a warmer room than my usual one, and still another produced a typewriter.

As a result of the disaster in Milan, I felt a warmth for the English people that has never wavered, and in Mrs. Dickins I found the friend of a lifetime. After her son William, my friend, died in a mountaineering accident, I became something like another son. She was one of my teachers, especially of art and poetry, and had an unerring ability to discover what in works of art makes them masterpieces.

I rewrote the dissertation. A friend who had read the first draft said it was much improved. Of course, he may have said this to comfort me, but I think he was probably right. All in all, I should have thanked the thief in Milan.

At this time I was asked by Eric Ceadel, the senior lecturer in Japanese, to teach Japanese conversation. This was my first experience teaching. At the time, students at Cambridge who knew no Japanese were introduced to the language by reading the preface to the tenth-century anthology of poetry *Kokinshū* in the original. It seemed strange to me to start learning a living language from a text a thousand years old, but the tradition of studying dead languages—Greek and Latin—was strong in England. Those trained in the classical languages found no problem in approaching Japanese as if it were a dead language.

My conversation classes were most peculiar. The students tended to use tenth-century vocabulary even when relating contemporary events. But my Japanese was suspect as well, as I hadn't spoken it in three years. I had become the teacher of conversation because there was not one Japanese in Cambridge.

I also attended the lectures on philosophy given by Bertrand Russell. This was his last year of teaching at Cambridge, and the class was very large. After one lecture, I went up to him with one of his books and asked him to sign it, offering my pen. He then used the pen to sign the books of the other students who also wanted his autograph. When he had finished, he realized he had kept me waiting and apologized. He invited me to have a beer with him. I was enchanted. We drank together until he had to leave for dinner, at which time he said, "Young man, I enjoy talking with you. Let us have beer together after every lecture this term." Someone who saw me walking down the street alongside Lord Russell said that he had never seen anyone look so happy.

Lord Russell spoke an English reminiscent of the eighteenth century in both vocabulary and wit. I remember his asking once if I had had a love affair. He added, "I won't be shocked even if you haven't." I wish I had written down all his conversations, but only one anecdote survives in a letter I wrote at the time. It was about a young Chinese whom Lord Russell had known. The man's teacher in China was known for his wisdom and also for never having taken a bath. When he died, someone suggested that his body be bathed, but the young man said, "No, bury him whole!"

I also got to know the novelist E. M. Forster. One of my teachers at Columbia, Lionel Trilling, who had written a book about Forster, gave me a letter of introduction. Forster was rather shy. Probably fearing we might lack mutual subjects of conversation, whenever he invited me for sherry he always invited someone from India or China so that I would have an Asian with whom to talk. But when he discovered we shared a passion for opera, he ceased worrying about topics of conversation.

On one occasion Forster invited several Americans to celebrate Thanksgiving. I had so much to drink that on the way back I fell off my bicycle, and because the wheel had gotten twisted out of shape, I had to carry the bicycle the rest of the way home. My remembrances of Cambridge almost always include a bicycle.

16

While living in Cambridge I traveled fairly often to London, an hour and a half away by train. London was a city filled with bombed-out sites. In Tokyo I had seen complete devastation, but in London even if a building had been hit and destroyed by German bombs, the neighboring buildings usually remained standing, though sometimes missing part of a wall. Although most of the famous buildings had survived the bombing, the British Museum was damaged. But most of its treasures had been removed to places of safety during the war, so the empty galleries were gloomy, with basins on the floors to catch water leaking from the ceiling. One gallery had been restored, though. It was filled with magnificent paintings, a reminder of the wealth of art in Britain and a promise that one day the museum's treasures would be visible again.

Not far from the British Museum was Gordon Square, where Arthur Waley lived. Waley had been my inspiration for years—the great translator who had rendered *The Tale of Genji* into marvelously beautiful English. He had translated not only Japanese but also Chinese works. I too had studied Chinese along with Japanese and hoped to become the second Waley. Unfortunately, this did not happen. The study of Japanese literature was all I could manage, and my knowledge of Chinese gradually faded away.

Various people had told me that it was difficult to keep a conversation going with Waley. If he was bored, he did not take pains to conceal it. A friend related that on one occasion, when Waley had a particularly tedious visitor, he took two books from his shelf and invited the visitor to go with him to the park in Gordon Square and, seated on separate benches, read a book. Even though it did not take Waley long to decide whether or not it was worth conversing with another person, he was not the kind of snob who was interested only in important people. On the contrary, he had such a wide variety of acquaintants that he might be described as a collector of unusual people. If I happened to inform an Australian clavichordist or a group of Javanese dancers or a Swiss ski teacher that I taught Japanese literature, I might be asked if I knew Arthur Waley, a friend of theirs.

Waley was a genius. The word *genius* is sometimes used in Japan for any foreigner who can read Japanese, but Waley knew not only Japanese and Chinese but also Sanskrit, Mongol, and the principal European languages. Moreover, he knew these languages not as a linguist interested mainly in words and grammar but as a man with an unbounded interest in the literature, history, and religion of every part of the world. He loved poetry written in the languages he knew, and if he did not know a language that was reputed to have good poetry, he did not begrudge the time needed to learn it. Late in life he learned Portuguese in order to read the poetry of a young friend.

The first time I met Waley was when he gave a lecture in Cambridge on the Ainu epic poems (*yukar*). It was typical of Waley, then in his sixties, to have learned Ainu for the pleasure of translating poetry written in a language that hardly a hundred scholars in the entire world were able to read. His beautiful translation of the Ainu epic totally changed my uneducated impressions of that people.

Waley had very high standards and was not given to flattery. When I sent him my translation of a Yuan drama, he returned it with the comment, "Have you ever written poetry of your own?" I interpreted this as a crushing evaluation of my attempts to translate the lyrical parts of the play into English verse. But this only made his praise, when it came, all the more precious. Although he seldom communicated directly to me his opinion of my work, I learned from the friends I introduced to Waley—notably Nagai Michio and Mishima Yukio—of the warmth with which he had spoken of me.

I knew hardly anyone else in London, but I went there when I could, especially for concerts and operas. I marvel now that I was able to hear so much music with so little money. It was a brilliant period for music in London. Musicians from the Continent who had been unable to visit England during the war years appeared in a steady stream. Some (like the great Norwegian soprano Kirsten Flagstad) had been celebrated even before the war; others like Elizabeth Schwartzkopf and Victoria de los Angeles, though unknown when they arrived in London, quickly became famous.

At that time, all operas were sung in English except during a brief international season in June. Sometimes if a singer was unable to sing his role in English, he was permitted to sing it in another language, though this made for peculiar dialogue onstage. I remember a performance of *Boris Godunov* during which Boris Christoff sang in impassioned Russian and everybody else in well-behaved English. Nobody in the audience seemed to mind the difference in styles.

If I had to choose the three most memorable performances I attended at this time, one would certainly be *Boris Godunov.* Christoff was so much absorbed by his role as the czar tortured by his conscience that he took even his curtain calls gravely, in character. Another was *Salome* with Ljuba Welitsch. In the production by Salvador Dalí, all the singers were costumed and masked to look like birds, and at the end the whole set turned into a huge peacock. Welitsch, however, refused to appear as a bird. Instead, she wore a bright red wig and a brilliant green costume. She sang superbly and her dance was sensationally erotic. Finally, there was the greatest performance of my whole operagoing career, Maria Callas in *Norma.* This performance has been preserved on records, but it would be impossible to guess from the sound alone the excitement caused by a wonderful singer who brought dramatic conviction to every note and gesture. I heard Callas sing later at the Metropolitan in New York, and each performance was a revelation, but I never again was so deeply moved as by *Norma.* Perhaps such an experience can happen only once.

Looking back on my long career as an operagoer from the time at seventeen when I saw opera from the last row of the top balcony at the Metropolitan, I recall these London performances with particular affection and with gratitude that I happened to be present during an extraordinary revival of music. At the same time, it comes to me as a shock when I confess to myself that despite my love of nō, bunraku, kabuki, and other forms of Japanese theater, something inside me craves opera and responds to it as to no other theater.

The music I heard in postwar London was not confined to operas. I remember especially the first performance of Richard Strauss's *Four Last Songs*, sung by Kirsten Flagstad. It is exciting to be present when a work of art is given its first performance, though often the first performance is also the last. In this instance, however, there could be no doubt from the first hearing that these songs would be sung and remembered for many years if not forever. After the performance I wandered the streets aimlessly, unable to think of anything else.

I recall London during my years in England in terms of Waley and music rather than of sightseeing. I dutifully visited the Tower of London and Westminster Abbey and walked along the Thames, but I did not search for the houses of famous English writers of the past. I did not have a favorite restaurant (the food was almost as tasteless there as in Cambridge), nor did I look for antiques or books. Somehow London did not then exert the spell over me that Paris did, though today there are few cities in the world I like as much. I no doubt have changed, but so has London. It is easier now for me to appreciate its solid splendor.

On the whole I was happy during the five years I lived in England. Although sometimes I was lonely, I believed that loneliness was unavoidable in a scholar's life. I enjoyed my solitary hours in the university library, reading whatever Japanese books happened to catch my attention. I still kept hoping for a chance to go to Japan, but none seemed likely to come my way. Apart from the restrictions imposed by the Occupation authorities on visiting scholars, there was the problem of money. Although my salary was sufficient for me to live reasonably well in Cambridge, buying an airplane ticket to Japan was far beyond my means.

During the summer of 1952 I returned to Columbia to take part in making translations for *Sources of Japanese Tradition*, the book based on Tsunoda-sensei's lectures on Japanese thought that Ted de Bary was editing. I took advantage of being in New York to visit foundations that might grant me a fellowship to study in Japan. But the foundation officers I met were discouraging. One told me frankly that if two candidates for a fellowship had about equal merits, he would choose the one whose field was a modern discipline—economics, sociology, or something equally important in the modern world—and not a specialist in literature.

In the hopes of pleasing such foundation officers, I drew up a proposal to study modern Japanese literature with a focus on its indebtedness to classical literature. Even though this was not what I really wanted to study—the life and poetry of Bashō—I was willing to compromise in order to go to Japan.

To my surprise, I received a fellowship, perhaps because I had stressed the modernity of my planned study. Now that I knew I could go to Japan, it occurred to me that I probably would never again have enough money to visit other countries on the way to Japan. I decided, therefore, to see as much of Asia as I could.

My ticket from London scheduled stops in Egypt, India, Ceylon (Sri Lanka), Singapore, Indonesia, Thailand, Cambodia, Hong Kong, and, finally, Japan. Getting visas took time and patience, but eventually my passport was stamped with the necessary permissions to visit these nine countries.

There were, however, unexpected modifications to my plans. The plane could not land in Cairo because anti-British riots threatened the airport. So it went instead to Basra, Iraq, where we stayed at the airline hotel. In those days planes did not fly at night, and each major airline had a hotel where passengers spent the night. Once we were settled in the hotel, I felt reluctant to visit an exotic country without seeing the sights.

So I arranged with a taxi driver to take me around the city, and an Australian couple joined me. Very soon the heat inside the car became so intolerable that we lost all interest in the city. Although we asked the driver to take us back to the hotel immediately, he was determined to get the full amount we had arranged for the tour, and he drove with maddening slowness along totally uninteresting streets. The only thing I can remember of Basra is seeing men slitting dates, removing the pits with their teeth, and then putting the dates in oval boxes destined for England. This was my first glimpse of the part of Asia farthest from Japan.

I did not know anyone in India, but I had the name of an inexpensive hotel in Bombay. The drive from the airport in an ancient taxi, a relic of the British occupation, was an introduction to an unfamiliar world. Concrete buildings along the streets, though of recent construction according to the dates inscribed on them, already were stained with large patches of mold, and in their shadow were innumerable cots on which people spent the night. Crowds of men passed by, their faces gaunt and the expression in their eyes almost desperately intense.

My most memorable encounter with an Indian during my journey was at Mount Abu, a site sacred to the Jain religion. The old guidebook I consulted said that the lake should not be missed. In the hotel restaurant I asked a waiter how to get to the lake, but hearing my question, a man seated at a nearby table answered, "In the days when the British were here the lake was lovely, but God in his mercy did not see fit for the British to make this a decent place for human beings to live, and now the lake is not worth seeing." This opinion, definitely not typical of most Indians, delighted me because it was so unexpected. I enjoyed talking with Indians because they were not afraid to voice even the most unpopular views.

Like other incautious travelers in India, I was plagued by diarrhea. Even though I resolved not to allow this to keep me from my sightseeing, again and again while in the midst of admiring sculptures in a museum or conversing with people on a train, I had to make a sudden dash for the nearest convenience.

Each of the countries I visited on my journey to Japan was memorable, but the summit was Cambodia. I stayed at the Grand Hotel, an edifice that in more peaceful times must have accommodated hundreds of guests. There were only four guests, however, at the time of my visit—a Belgian with his Russian wife, a Polish mathematician who taught at Columbia, and me. At first we maintained our distance in the huge dining room, but before long the barriers of reserve fell and we went everywhere together. Travel was in pedicabs—rickshaws pulled by a man on a bicycle—the typical means of travel throughout Southeast Asia.

Angkor Wat, Bayon, and the nearby sites constitute what for me is the most splendid group of buildings in the world. The Taj Mahal is perhaps more perfect, the lonely temples of Pagan in Burma more conducive to reveries, and the Great Wall of China more evocative of history, but the combination of architecture and sculptures at Angkor makes it unique.

There was no warfare in Cambodia at the time of my visit, but early in the morning the hotel personnel drilled with wooden guns. One day Prince Sihanouk came to the hotel, and the four foreigners watched from a respectful distance as he delivered an impassioned address in Cambodian, unable to understand whether he was calling for greater friendship with the West or for the expulsion of all foreigners.

The Polish mathematician and I traveled from Angkor to the capital, Phnom Penh, aboard what was called a "native bus."

The bus had no sides. This may have been convenient for getting off, but every time the bus rounded a curve, it seemed likely a few of the passengers would be thrown out. Phnom Penh was quiet, and the museum was full of wonderful sculptures, but we were advised that when we went to a restaurant to choose a table as far from the door as possible, as it was quite common for passing terrorists to toss bombs into public buildings.

The one country where I had acquaintances was Indonesia. All my friends were the descendants of Chinese who had emigrated to Java hundreds of years before. They knew Indonesian, of course, but normally they spoke Dutch, the language of the colonizers, and were graduates of Dutch schools. Their most Chinese characteristic was their absorption with food. Every trip to a monument was planned in terms of where we would eat lunch.

Sightseeing had an element of danger. One never knew when a soldier stopped the car if he was really a member of the Indonesian army or a bandit dressed in an army uniform. Whenever my friends left the city, they went in a battered car, not their city car, so as not to attract the attention of bandits. Indeed, the fear of bandits extended to every part of life. At night the rooms in my friend's house were separately locked so that even if a robber managed to get into one room he would be unable to penetrate the others.

Bribery was the other face of the general disorder. My friend did not receive the telegram I had sent from Singapore because he did not pay a bribe to the post office. When he complained that he could not live on his salary, the minister of education asked him why he did not take bribes.

Despite such inconveniences, I remember Indonesia in 1953 with nostalgia. I recall with particular pleasure a palace where girls performed Javanese dances. I had seen similar dances in New York, but the effect was totally different. I felt something sad and beautiful in the dances, as if I were witnessing the end of a epoch, a time when there were dancers and musicians in a prince's household. When I reached Japan and told people of my experiences in Indonesia, most opined that it was just like Japan in the early Meiji era. I did not agree.

I arrived at Tokyo's Haneda (the old Haneda) airport on a rainy night in August 1953, and I took a bus into the city. At the railway station I bought a second-class ticket to Kyoto, the last train that night. I also sent a telegram to Yokoyama Masakatsu, a friend from Qingdao, now living in Kyoto, announcing my arrival the next day.

The train obviously dated from before the war. The seats were uncomfortable, and there was no air conditioning. When I started to fan myself with an old letter, the man sitting in front of me took out a fan from his briefcase and gave it to me, the first act of kindness I received on arriving in Japan. The picture on the fan was by Yokoyama Taikan, the one modern Japanese painter whose name I knew.

I fell asleep at some point, though generally I am quite unable to sleep on a train or plane. When I awoke and looked out, I saw that the train had stopped at Sekigahara Station. The name sent a thrill through me. Tokyo had seemed very much like a European city, especially after Southeast Asia, but the name Sekigahara was proof that I definitely was in Japan. I had, of course, described the battle of Sekigahara when I wrote about the Tokugawa period and when I taught Japanese history at Cambridge. I had also wondered how Japan might have developed if the Tokugawa forces had not been victorious. At Sekigahara Station early one August morning I felt for the first time contact with Japanese history.

Mr. Yokoyama met me at Kyoto Station. He was surprised that I had not spent a night in Tokyo before continuing my journey, but after a month or more without studying, I was eager to reach my destination and to open my books.

Mr. Yokoyama took me to his house in the northern part of the city, at the foot of Mount Kinugasa. He assumed that I would be tired and want to rest, but I was too excited to think of resting. I was eager to see Kyoto, anything at all, and when he told me he had to go that afternoon to Yamazaki where he had an appointment at the Suntory Distillery, I asked to be taken along. This was my first sightseeing excursion in Kyoto. When Mr. Yokoyama introduced me to Mr. Torii, the president of the company, he mentioned that I had escorted the crown prince when he visited Cambridge in June. Mr. Torii, greatly pleased, gave me a bottle of whiskey with the Imperial crest impressed into the glass. (The contents vanished not long afterward when Mr. Yokoyama took me to his favorite bar.)

That night we walked along Ponto-chō. It was so beautiful I could hardly believe my eyes. All the buildings on both sides of

this narrow lane were in Japanese style. There were lanterns at each door, and along the lane walked apprentice geishas wearing kimonos whose gold thread glittered in the dark. Ponto-chō seemed like the other face of Sekigahara, the feminine side of Japanese culture. That night it was magical, and it is sad to see how it has been defaced in recent years.

The next day I took out my copy of Bashō's haiku. I had decided I would study in the mornings and go sightseeing in the afternoons. However, on the first morning I had trouble studying because of the noise emanating from the kindergarten next door. Looking for a quieter place, I found my way to Tōji-in, a few minutes' walk away. The temple then became my regular place for studying, as it was virtually deserted. Although a few young men, studying for their college entrance examinations, lived there, I never saw a priest or a tourist.

One of the first things I published in Japanese was an account of the Reikō-den at the Tōji-in, the hall sacred to the successive Ashikaga shoguns. With a touch of exaggeration, I observed that it was chilly there even at the height of summer. The two rows of wooden statues of the Ashikaga shoguns, their eyes glittering in the dark, make an imposing and even frightening presence.

The Ryōan-ji was also nearby. While at the Navy Language School, I had heard of this temple's famous sand and stone garden, and it did not disappoint me. Occasionally tourists came, but somehow the unadorned beauty of the stones and the raked sand silenced the exclamations one expects from tourists. I remember best one night when I went to see the garden by moonlight. As I gazed at the stones and sand, probably not thinking cosmic thoughts, I heard a faint noise beside me. I looked over and saw that the wife of the priest of the temple had placed a cup of tea beside me. We talked for a while. She told me that she had been sent to America as a picture bride, but the marriage had not taken place. I asked what she remembered of America. She said she had climbed a tall mountain, even taller than Mount Hiei.

Kyoto—indeed, all of Japan—lingers in my memory most vividly in terms of the people I met—not only those who became friends but even persons I hardly knew who showed me kindness, like the priest's wife at Ryōan-ji. Even though these memories remain unchanged, much of Kyoto has been destroyed by greed or the passion for convenience. The last time I visited the Ryōan-ji, perhaps twenty years ago, I was appalled by the number of tourist buses parked in front and by the motorcycles zooming in and out of the temple precincts. No doubt some people are pleased with the change, rejoicing that Ryōan-ji is now open to everyone, but can the tourists who leave the buses for the ten minutes allotted to the temple appreciate the stillness of the place? I anticipate with dismay that one day there will be a display of sound and light in the garden, the stones shifting in colors from purple to orange to the tune of koto music.

When I was first in Kyoto, people who had known the city before the war would tell me how it had been ruined by change. Such talk was profoundly irritating to me. I loved the city as I knew it, and I did not wish to be informed how much better Kyoto was in the days of gasoline rationing. Even though gasoline was not rationed in 1953, I believe that there was not one privately owned car in the city. Of course, there were taxis and three-wheeled vehicles, but traffic was light. I remember seeing two elderly ladies who, as they crossed each other's path in the middle of Kawara-machi, removed their coats before bowing. Today, an unending tide of oncoming vehicles does not permit such etiquette.

People in Kyoto are apt to take pride not in the number of temples and gardens that survive from the past but in the fact that the first streetcars in Japan ran in their city, that three major Japanese department stores had their beginnings in Kyoto, and that the aqueduct that brings water from Lake Biwa to the city is the oldest in Japan. There is surprisingly little local pride in a place that, more than anywhere else in Japan, should arouse this emotion. On occasion, there have been demonstrations against the mutilation of the city, but they generally have been organized by foreigners.

It is easy for me to feel irritated when I return to Kyoto after a year's absence and see the latest destruction. Of course, there still are places that preserve the beauty of the past. One can sit for hours in the Lecture Hall of the Tōji and admire the incredible display of Buddhas without having to listen to musical accompaniment. One can find streets where people still make objects by hand. In the summer one can dine on *yuka* (platforms erected along the Kamo River) and watch the ducks. One can find everywhere monuments to the past, ranging from the glory of the Heian period to the chaos of the era preceding the Meiji Restoration. It is a marvelous city, even with its wounds.

I think of myself as being extremely lucky to have seen Kyoto when I did. Probably students from abroad who live in Kyoto today, not missing the beauty I remember, feel equally lucky to see the city. But one can anticipate only further damage, more wooden buildings replaced by concrete structures, more quiet bookstores turned into display cases for garish best sellers, but the hills and the rivers will remain.

I think that if I could un-invent one feature of modern life, it would be the car. How wonderful Kyoto would be if there were no cars! Anyone who has spent time in Venice knows what spiritual succor comes from the quiet of a city without cars, where the only sounds are of people's footsteps. At the risk of being called a reactionary, I will shout, "Down with the car!"

Fifty years ago Kyoto was a wonderful city in which to walk. Every street had something that caught my attention—whether a tiny secondhand bookstore or a shop that sold nothing but badgers made of stone. I had been warned by Japanese friends, however, not to purchase pottery or other works of art until my eyes had become accustomed to Japanese taste. This was good advice and kept me from making mistakes at the beginning, when everything I saw seemed beautiful.

I was tempted most of all by books, and I sometimes found bargains. I bought, for example, a copy of the first volume of

Sasameyuki (*The Makioka Sisters*), privately printed during the war in an edition of two hundred copies in Hyōgo Prefecture, with a flyleaf inscribed with a poem and signature in Tanizaki's handwriting. It cost 750 yen, about two dollars at the time.

But this was unusual. I did not have much money to spend, and apart from the occasional rarity, I confined myself to buying books that seemed likely to be of use to me in my future research. I must have bought several hundred volumes, but in retrospect, this was a mistake. Most of the books I acquired at that time were printed on such poor-quality paper that the pages turn to powder if I touch them. In most cases, too, better editions of the texts have since appeared.

The things that were free were more precious than anything I could have bought. A visit to a temple, even one so lacking in fame that it was not on any tourist route, might produce an unforgettable impression. I remember, for example, my first visit to Seikan-ji. Its central divinity, a thousand-armed *kannon*, had lost many of its tiny hands, which had been collected in a dish in front of the statue. In any other country, people would surely have stolen them.

My happiness in Kyoto was in large part due to having an ideal place to live. Other foreign students were not always so fortunate during the early postwar years, having difficulty finding lodgings in private houses. No doubt the people of Kyoto, remembering the Occupation, were hesitant about having a foreigner under the same roof, though refusal was generally made in terms of the toilet's being dirty or something similar. A student of mine at Cambridge had been obliged to live for months in the bleak Hyakumanben Temple because, initially at least, no one else would take him in. But there was an exception: Nishida Shizuko, the daughter of the celebrated philosopher, took pity on foreign students and usually had several living in her house. When I visited the house, I would see huge clogs in the entrance.

At the time, there were only ten or twelve foreign students in Kyoto, including Burton Watson, then serving as an assistant to Professor Yoshikawa Kōjirō at Kyoto University. Even though Watson had acquired remarkable fluency in Japanese, his field was Chinese literature. He was unassuming and made light of his accomplishments, but he had already begun to develop into the finest translator of Chinese literature in the West. Once when I visited him, I discovered he was reading and typing a translation of *Records of the Grand Historian*, more or less simultaneously. I expressed my astonishment, but to him this seemed quite ordinary.

The foreign students in Kyoto met once a month or so in a Chinese restaurant. Most were Americans, but an Englishman and a Belgian were included as well. Gatherings of students abroad are apt to take the form of complaints about the country where they are studying, but I cannot recall any complaints about Kyoto. No doubt we sensed how lucky we were to live in this wonderful city. After dinner we often took a taxi to a coffee shop. We generally managed to get six passengers into a tiny Renault, the typical taxi, though this required two people to sit on someone's lap.

Apart from these gatherings, I almost never spoke English. I listened to Japanese radio, read Japanese newspapers, went to only Japanese films. There was one memorable exception. I went to see the American film of *Julius Caesar*. Although this is one of the plays of Shakespeare I like least, the sound of the poetry was intoxicating. When I left the theater, I was dazed, and I realized that however completely I gave myself to Japanese, something within me was stirred even more profoundly by the English language. But this was not necessarily to be regretted, as I would have to maintain my love of English if I were to recapture the beauty of Japanese texts in my translations.

Once in a while an American, bearing an introduction from a mutual friend, looked me up. This could be enjoyable and result in friendship, but more often it was exasperating. One visitor asked me to guide him to some famous places, so I took him to temples in the part of Kyoto I knew best—Ryōan-ji, Tōji-in, Ninna-ji, and so on. He seemed pleased, but after the third or fourth temple he asked, "Isn't there anything else to see except temples?" That was where the tour ended.

Even worse was the rich publisher who took me along as an interpreter when buying antiques. We went into several shops in Shinmonzen without his showing any interest, but eventually he found some metal figurines he liked. He asked how much they cost, and I interpreted. The shopkeeper stated the price. Apparently the publisher had been told that in the Orient it is necessary to haggle over prices. He therefore asked me to tell the shopkeeper that he was a poor American who could not afford to spend so much money. I interpreted, hating every word I had to say because I knew they were untrue. The shopkeeper explained that the objects were on consignment and that he could not reduce the price without consulting the owner. The publisher responded, "That's what they all say. He'll change his mind when we start to leave." Although the shopkeeper did not change the price, two days later, after the publisher had left the country, I had a telephone call saying that the owner of the figurines, touched by the interest of a poor American, was willing to cut the price. I felt so implicated in the matter that I had no choice but to buy the figurines.

But such interruptions in my normally happy life were infrequent and soon forgotten. My study at Kyoto University was in some ways a disappointment, but in the end it worked to my advantage. When I first visited the university and asked for a schedule of classes, I was told there was none. Someone then told me that the professor of Japanese literature would be offering a course but that it might not start for a couple of weeks. This vagueness was disconcerting, but I had done my duty to the Ford Foundation by registering at the university.

The first class I attended was in October. As far as I remember, there were only two or three additional classes during the rest of the year. The students would assemble at the assigned time and wait for the professor to appear. By November the classroom was cold, and there was no heating. For twenty or thirty minutes we sat on our hands to keep them warm until someone said, "It looks as if he is not coming today." Then we would get up and go home.

Later I discovered why the professor so rarely appeared. The salaries paid to professors at national universities were so meager that he had no choice but to take additional teaching jobs elsewhere. But later on, when I had stopped attending class and saw the professor only in his office, he was extremely helpful and generous with his time.

As the result of this dispensation from attending classes, I was able to enjoy Kyoto without hindrance. I had a map with the names of the famous places circled and would set out every day to explore a still unknown site. I enjoyed walking on clogs and practiced until I could make the same kind of slurring sound as a Japanese, and I only once had the annoyance of a broken thong. But this recalled to me a similar scene in the novella *Takekurabe* (*Growing Up*), and I felt pleased to be having a truly Japanese experience. Clogs are the best conveyance on which to see Kyoto.

20

Living in Kyoto enabled me to learn, painlessly, much about Japanese history. I had formerly had difficulty, for example, remembering whether it was Yoshimitsu or Yoshimasa who built the Ginkaku-ji, but after actually visiting the temple and seeing Yoshimasa's statue, I never again confused the two shoguns.

I also learned much about myself. I had supposed that the test of a scholar's worth was whether or not something he had written was published by a learned journal. I was therefore delighted when an article I had written about Hirata Atsutane was accepted by T'oung Pao, then the most reputable journal of East Asian studies. Although I tried to make the article interesting, my objective was less to give readers pleasure than to present information. Probably not fifty people in the world ever read my article.

In Japan, by contrast, almost from the time I arrived, I was of interest to the press. Newspapers asked for articles, and I appeared on the radio. My first appearance in a Japanese magazine actually preceded my arrival. A book review I published in an American scholarly journal of Sasaki Nobutsuna's *Jōdai Nihon bungaku shi (A History of Ancient Japanese Literature)* was translated and published in *Bungaku* (without my permission). My review was unfavorable to Sasaki largely because I did not share his nationalism. In fact, I was irritated by the political convictions that caused him to praise any poem composed by an emperor. I concluded my review by declaring that scholars in the West would have to write their own histories of Japanese literature.

I did not expect that this review would be published in Japan. I recognized that Sasaki had contributed to the study of Japanese literature and feared that my harsh review might affect the health of an old man. I also feared that my conclusion might be interpreted as an assertion that any foreigner could write a better history of Japanese literature than Sasaki could.

The review did upset Sasaki, who wrote a letter expressing his profound devotion to the Imperial Household. He also mentioned (supposing I was British) his admiration for British scholarship ever since the days of the great Basil Hall Chamberlain.

This disagreeable incident led, however, to my becoming friends with Tamai Kensuke, the editor of *Bungaku*. Some months later he asked me to write an article on the translations of *The Tale of Genji*. This was the first article I had ever written in Japanese. Although I was aware from newspapers and magazines that almost nobody used old *kana* orthography and unabbreviated Chinese characters any longer, I nevertheless chose to write the unabbreviated characters in the manner I had learned at the Japanese Language School. But Tamai, like virtually every other editor for whom I wrote at the time, converted my text into the new *kana* orthography.

My article on *The Tale of Genji* was colored by my enormous admiration for Arthur Waley's translation, which had meant so much to me in my life and as a scholar of Japan. It would have been better if I had contented myself with praising Waley, but in the effort to persuade Japanese readers of the merits of his translation, I stated that it was better than Tanizaki Jun'ichirō's translation. Not long afterward I met Tanizaki, the one living Japanese whose works I knew fairly well. After my article appeared, I wrote him a letter of apology, and he answered that the article had not bothered him. Of course not. Why should he have been concerned about what an unknown, young foreign student of Japanese literature thought of his translation? But I was impressed by his refusal to take offense.

The third article I wrote for *Bungaku* was a review that Tamai requested of a book entitled *Nihon bungaku no koten* (*Classics of Japanese Literature*), a Marxist interpretation of Japanese literature. I was, of course, familiar with the Marxism and anti-Americanism that was so popular at the time. Every month I looked over the table of contents of three *sōgō zasshi* (general-interest magazines), and sometimes I read the articles. Hardly an issue was without at least one exposé of the menace of American monopolistic capitalism. But this was my first encounter with Marxism in discussions of the classics of Japanese literature, and I was dismayed. The book did not mention *Kokinshū* because it was written by aristocrats and not by the common people. *The*

Tale of Genji was depicted as a revelation of contradictions in the ruling class. Other works were praised or condemned depending on whether or not they were "democratic."

My review was not published for several months, and when it appeared, it was accompanied by a counterreview by one of the three authors. He dismissed my review as an unsolicited contribution, although Tamai surely remembered that he had requested it. The reviewer went on to accuse me of being a *kizokuteki puchiburoteki fuhaishita seiyōjin* (aristocratic, petty bourgeois, decadent Westerner). When I recall this now, I find it amusing, but I was not amused at the time. I hoped someone would answer the accusations leveled against me, but no one did. Nagai Michio advised me to ignore the attack, and he was right. It was the price I had to pay for leaving the secluded world of academic publications and taking part in hurly-burly of journalism.

My greatest pleasure at this time was my *kyōgen* (comic drama) lessons. It had occurred to me that I would understand Japanese culture better if I learned a traditional art. After thinking over the various possibilities, I chose *kyōgen*. Although I had been deeply impressed by nō, I was attracted by the language of *kyōgen* and felt it would be more fun. When my landlady made inquiries about a *kyōgen* teacher, the head of the Kyoto branch of the Ōkura school, learning of my interest, decided to delegate his son, Shigeyama Sennojō, as the teacher of the first foreigner to study *kyōgen*.

I thoroughly enjoyed my weekly *kyōgen* lessons. They took place in my house, which was so far removed from the neighbors that no one would be disturbed by the loud voices used in declaiming *kyōgen* dialogue. My attempts to imitate Sennojō were a novel experience. Before this, my education had been through my eyes, but now I was learning entirely with my ears. Unlike my experience when I performed in high school plays and was urged to imagine I was a servant or a prince, I now had no need of imagination. It was incumbent on me to imitate

Sennojō's voice as closely as possible. Only if one has become an accomplished *kyōgen* actor is it permissible to "break the mold." In fact, far from inhibiting me, the insistence on imitating my teacher gave me pleasure. I felt as if I had found a place at the end of a long line of predecessors.

Occasionally the lessons took place elsewhere. I felt self-conscious in my *haori* and *hakama* (traditional Japanese male attire) when I left the house, resolved not to notice if people stared at me. On one occasion a group of young men jogging stopped in their tracks to stare in astonishment. But I soon realized that if I disliked being stared at, I had no business taking up a performing art.

The height of my short career as a *kyōgenshi* was as Tarōkaja in *Chidori* at the Kita Nōgakudō on September 13, 1956. The role of the owner of the saké shop was taken by Takechi Tetsuji, known especially for his "Takechi Kabuki." A video about five minutes long survives of part of the performance. (At the time video film was extremely expensive and was used parsimoniously.) When I see it now I can hardly believe I am the person delivering the lines, gesturing, jumping up and down, and finally exiting to the words *onma ga mairu* (His Excellency's horse is on the way). Even more unbelievable is the audience visible in the video, including Tanizaki Jun'ichirō, Kawabata Yasunari, Mishima Yukio, Matsumoto Kōshirō, and other famous people. It was my only triumph on the stage.

21

Once I had settled down in my wonderful lodgings in Ima-kumano, I decided I would spend mornings reading the works of Bashō and afternoons exploring the historical sites in Kyoto. This would have been an economical use of my precious time in

Japan, but several unforeseen developments compelled me to alter this plan.

The first occurred a few weeks after I moved to the detached cottage in Imakumano. Mrs. Okumura, the owner, informed me that an assistant professor at Kyoto University, just returned from America, would be moving into a room on the ground floor of the main house. The news was most unwelcome. I felt sure that the assistant professor would want to practice his English on me. Or perhaps he would regale me with reminiscences of his life in America. I decided to avoid him, though this was somewhat difficult because I had to pass his room every time I went out.

After he moved in, I was careful whenever I went by his room. I would gaze up at the sky or down at my feet, though I might be aware from the corner of my eyes that he was eating a soft-boiled egg. One day Mrs. Okumura, who prepared meals for both of us, said apologetically that she had visitors that evening and would like me to eat dinner that night with the assistant professor. I agreed, though with a little annoyance.

That evening the assistant professor, Nagai Michio, and I had dinner in the cottage. I don't remember what we talked about, but I felt greatly attracted to his warm personality. It also gave me pleasure to discuss intellectual matters in Japanese. For his part, Nagai-san seems to have enjoyed talking with an American who had come to Japan to learn rather than to boast of American know-how. In any case, we decided that henceforth we would have dinner together every evening.

I had made a friend for life. Although Nagai-san was a year younger than I, I looked up to him as a teacher, my first and best guide to Japan. A month earlier, when Mrs. Okumura asked me which newspaper I would take, I had replied that I had no time to read newspapers. This was foolish, but I was determined to learn as much as possible about Japanese literature during my one year in Kyoto, and I thought that an hour spent mulling over haiku by

Bashō was a better use of my time than reading a newspaper. But as the result of my nightly conversations with Nagai-san, I came to realize that I could not ignore the living culture of Japan. Arthur Waley had refused invitations to visit Japan because his interest was in the Japan of the Heian period and not in the present. Although I shared his absorption with the past, under Nagai-san's influence I not only began to read newspapers but actually came to want to participate in Japanese life.

I joined a group devoted to studying the Japanese traditional arts, especially the theater. As a result of their country's defeat in the war, many Japanese had come to doubt or even totally reject their traditional culture. People freely predicted that nō would soon disappear because it was no longer of relevance. This was true not only of nō but of bunraku (puppet plays) as well. In fact, the audiences at bunraku performances in Osaka usually numbered only forty or fifty people, despite this being a golden age of performance. So in an attempt to win new audiences for bunraku, even *Hamlet* and *Madame Butterfly* were made into puppet plays. I remember another play whose hero was a noble dog, and still another that ended with a half–African American child, scorned by his classmates because of his color, standing in a snowstorm in hopes of becoming white.

Rejection of the past was not restricted to the theater. The celebrated essay by Kuwabara Takeo, a professor at Kyoto University, characterizing haiku as a second-class art had caused many poets to give up not only haiku but also *tanka* (thirty-one-syllable poems). Painting in any Japanese style was dismissed as merely decorative. Action painting was in vogue. I even read about one painter who set in motion a toy truck that spattered paint at random over the canvas, creating a work of truly abstract art.

I could understand the eagerness of young Japanese to shake off the burden of traditions that had choked the freedom to experiment and develop in new directions, but it made me sad that nō, bunraku, and haiku might soon become obsolete. I had received a fellowship from the Ford Foundation to examine the survival of traditional themes in modern literature, but there seemed little chance I would find anything of significance. By general agreement, the best hope for invigorating Japanese tradition was Kinoshita Junji's *Yūzuru* (*Twilight Crane*). It was successful not only as a modern play but also as an opera and even as a nō play. Members of the study group referred to *Yūzuru* again and again in their discussions of how to preserve Japanese tradition.

At first I enjoyed these sessions and the members were always friendly, but I got the impression that they were interested in me not as an individual but as a representative of all the non-Japanese in the world. I was rarely asked what I thought of some work of art. Instead, I was asked what people abroad thought of it, and in the end, I stopped attending the meetings. It was much more satisfactory talking with Nagai Michio.

The first time I traveled from Kyoto to Tokyo, Nagai-san gave me an introduction to Shimanaka Hōji, a friend of his from childhood. The offices of Shimanaka's publishing company, Chūō kōron sha, were opposite Tokyo Station. After reading the note from Nagai-san, Shimanaka-san spoke courteously, asking how he might help me. At first I did not detect in him the warmth that emanated from Nagai-san, but in time he became just as close a friend. To have lost them both (though both were younger than me) was a blow from which I shall not recover.

When I described to Shimanaka-san the project for which I had received a fellowship, he said that Kinoshita Junji was the best author to consult and at once arranged for a meeting. This was typical of my relationship with Shimanaka over the years to come. He always knew the right person to meet, the right book to consult, the right scholar to decide some academic problem.

The meeting with Kinoshita was in every way agreeable, and I was grateful for his willingness to spend time with an unknown foreign scholar, but we disagreed on one point. He had successfully used traditional folklore materials in such works as *Yūzuru*, but he was not interested in creating works based on the aristocratic traditions of the past. This was a disappointment. I had hoped that he might write a play based, say, on the legend of Ono no Komachi. Although I did not know it at the time, but the next writer to whom Shimanaka-san would introduce me, Mishima Yukio, had already written a "modern nō play" about Komachi.

Shimanaka-san also suggested that I write for *Chūō kōron*. I had known the name of this periodical from wartime days when the intelligence office in Honolulu received word that the Japanese government had banned its publication. Although I did not know why the magazine had been banned, I assumed that it must have opposed the militarists' policies. It thus was a great honor to be asked to write for so distinguished a journal. Although I did not actually begin to write for *Chūō kōron* until January 1955, that year I published six articles.

I wrote these articles in Japanese as an expression of my desire to participate in Japanese society. Shimanaka-san read over my manuscript before it was published, to make sure that there were no mistakes in my Japanese. However, he left certain phrases as they were, even though they were not normal Japanese, in the hope that they might stimulate Japanese writers into using fresh expressions.

The articles were later put together to form the book *Aoi ne no Tarōkaja* (*The Blue-Eyed Tarōkaja*), the nickname I had received because of my *kyōgen* appearances. When I read it today, it comes as a surprise that Tanizaki Jun'ichirō graciously supplied a preface. I am surprised also by how little my views have basically changed, though I have grown more tolerant. Recently, when I read over an article entitled "A Protest Against Preconceptions of Foreigners," I realized that today I am more likely to smile rather than protest when someone with an extremely common Japanese name such as Tanaka or Yamamoto hands me his card and expresses amazement that I, who have studied Japanese for only sixty years, can read the name, even if he fails to write the pronunciation in roman letters.

I enjoyed my first year in Kyoto so much that I was extremely reluctant to leave. So I wrote Cambridge University asking if I might remain in Japan another year, but my request was refused. Just at this time I had an offer from Columbia University, and no objection was raised to my spending an additional year in Japan. This settled matters; I resigned from Cambridge. I have sometimes regretted this decision, especially when I have returned to Cambridge for a visit and seen again its extraordinary beauty. But probably I made the right choice.

My second year in Kyoto was even more fruitful than the first. I compiled the two volumes of my *Anthology of Japanese Literature,* a work that exercised considerable influence on the next generation of foreign scholars of Japanese literature. I met many Japanese writers and read widely in modern literature for the first time. I became friends with some writers, especially Mishima Yukio, a relationship that continued unbroken until his death. I saw Tanizaki on numerous occasions. I cannot say I became his friend—we were too far apart in age and accomplishments—but I enjoyed being invited to his house. On one occasion Shiga Naoya was a fellow guest at dinner. I wish I had made notes on the conversation that night, but it never occurred to me I would forget a word.

In Tokyo I met a couple who would figure very importantly in my life during the following years. The husband, Faubion Bowers, is credited with having, as a member of the Occupation, saved kabuki from zealous American censors who wished to remove every "feudal" element. He had returned to Japan to write a book comparing theater in Tokyo and New York. His wife, Santha Rama Rau, was the daughter of the first Indian ambassador to Japan. Her books were popular in America, and one had been translated into Japanese. Faubion obtained tickets for me to attend kabuki and introduced me to many kabuki actors. The three of us got along well, and we agreed when they left Japan that we would meet at Madurai in the south of India.

Leaving Japan was painful, as I was sure I would never again have enough money to visit. On the plane I read *Sumidagawa* (*The River Sumida*) by Nagai Kafū and was moved to tears by the beauty of the language.

As planned, I met Faubion and Santha in Madurai. They had rented a car and were going to travel up the east coast, eventually branching off to Delhi. With them was a photographer whom we came to detest because of his tedious jokes, but this drew the rest of us all the closer. We spent the nights in government hostels that were hot and uncomfortable. The food generally was terrible. In addition to these normal hardships of travel, we were burdened by the photographer's presence, and the journey took us through the least populated, bleakest parts of India. All the same, I have the impression we laughed the whole week long.

I returned to England to arrange to send my books from Cambridge to New York. The Bowers reached New York ahead of me, and they immediately took me into their circle of friends. I should have been too busy to see much of them, as it was my first year of teaching at Columbia and I had to prepare new lectures in Japanese literature and history. I also was translating Dazai Osamu's novel *Shayō* (*The Setting Sun*). Nevertheless, I spent four or five nights a week with the Bowers, often going with them to the theater or the opera. They always bought an extra ticket for me.

Sometimes I attended "celebrity parties" at their apartment. Faubion told me how he assembled such famous people. The trick was to secure one celebrity's willingness to attend. This done, one had merely to say "So-and-so is coming" to attract other celebrities. At first I was nervous at such parties, as I had never before met anyone in America who qualified as a celebrity. The conversations I had with these people were rarely of intrinsic interest, and I saw few of the celebrities more than once, but it is agreeable to recall having met them, though almost all are now dead.

Undoubtedly the most memorable celebrity I met was Greta Garbo. She was a close friend of Jane Gunther, the wife of the famous journalist John Gunther. Jane, an extremely intelligent and well-read woman, had accompanied John on his travels all over the world. When they met Nikita Khrushchev in Moscow, his first comment was to ask if all American men had such beautiful wives. Jane introduced Garbo to the Bowers and later to me.

Although Garbo had been retired for many years, she still was remembered as the greatest of all film actresses. One day I had a telephone call from Jane asking if I would take Garbo to the theater. Of course I eagerly accepted. The play was *The Diary of Anne Frank*. Before it began, Garbo hardly spoke, and during the intermission she covered her face with the program. We left just before the play ended to avoid being noticed. After emerging from the theater, we waited briefly for a taxi, and the drivers of passing cars halted their vehicles for a better look at the famous face.

I saw Garbo once again, at Jane's house. Another guest was R. K. Narayan, the great Indian writer. Garbo sat at the end of a sofa not saying anything. Looking at her I could not help but realize that she was no longer beautiful. I remember particularly that her lipstick was smeared. (Jane told me that Garbo could not bear looking at her face in the mirror.) But when Narayan began to speak of his conversations with his late wife in the world of the dead, Garbo's interest was awakened, and for a while we saw again the face that had captivated the world.

At such gatherings I was of some interest to the celebrities because Japan had suddenly become popular. Even people who had always assumed that Japanese culture was no more than an imitation of Chinese culture changed their minds after seeing the Japanese house erected at the Museum of Modern Art and the exhibition of Japanese National Treasures in various American cities. Zen teachings, introduced about this time, also enjoyed popularity with intellectuals as a religion without a god. An even more important factor was the sudden vogue of Japanese films, which began with *Rashōmon*. People at cocktail parties who might otherwise have had trouble thinking of something to say to a professor of Japanese literature were eager to ask me questions now that Japan was fashionable.

The new interest of publishers in translations of modern Japanese literature was of direct relevance to me. This change in attitude was initiated by Harold Strauss, the editor in chief at Knopf, the most important American publisher of translated literature. He had learned some Japanese during the war and had made his way (with help) through a few novels.

Strauss was not a lovable person. He was overbearing and was apt to make such statements as "Translators are a dime a dozen." When Kawabata Yasunari's *Yukiguni* (*Snow Country*) did not sell, despite the fine translation by Edward Seidensticker, he declared he would not publish any more of Kawabata's "effete writings"; but when Kawabata received the Nobel Prize, Strauss changed his mind and published *Yama no oto* (*The Sound of the Mountain*). The night that Mishima committed suicide Strauss telephoned me to say he was now prepared to pay higher fees for translations.

Despite these failings, Strauss deserves the gratitude of everyone connected with modern Japanese literature. He commissioned the translation of *Kikyō* (*Homecoming*) by Osaragi Jirō, the first Japanese novel published in twenty-five years by an American company. This novel describes the rediscovery by a Japanese of his country's culture. But for most American readers, unfamiliar with that culture, the novel brought a discovery rather than a rediscovery. The next novel in the Knopf series, Tanizaki's *Tade kuu mushi* (*Some Prefer Nettles*), also describes a rediscovery of traditional Japan.

Other American publishers followed Knopf's example, some preferring less traditional works. This was perhaps the most lasting result of the "Japan boom" of the 1950s.

When I left Japan in 1955, I wept in the airplane at the thought I might never again have enough money to return. As a matter of fact, however, I have managed to spend at least a month in Japan every year since then. When the purchase of airplane tickets was beyond my means, I generally succeeded in obtaining the necessary funds from some organization. In 1956, for example, I received travel expenses from *Newsweek*, in return for which I wrote five or six articles about events in Japan. Only one of these articles was ever printed.

In 1957 I was chosen as a delegate to the PEN Club Congress held in Tokyo and Kyoto. I owed this honor to being the only member of the American PEN Club who could speak Japanese. It was my first such experience, and I was excited to meet and even to converse with writers whose works I had long known. It was an unusually brilliant congress. Famous writers who normally avoided such gatherings gladly accepted the invitation to attend, mainly because the site was Japan. Although many American writers had lived in Paris or London in the 1920s and 1930s and had published nostalgic accounts of their experiences, probably not one writer of importance had ever visited Tokyo. "Going abroad" meant going to Europe, so this made Japan, because of its unfamiliarity, an alluring destination.

The American delegation included John Steinbeck (who received the Nobel Prize a few years later), Ralph Ellison (the best-known African American novelist), John Dos Passos (whose novel *USA* was a great favorite of mine), and John Hersey (who had published a celebrated book on the dropping of the atomic bomb on Hiroshima). The British delegation, equally distinguished, included Stephen Spender, Angus Wilson, and Kathleen Raine. There were delegates from many countries, including refugees who described with bitterness what it meant to be exiles, forbidden to return to their own countries.

The Japanese delegation, naturally the most numerous, was headed by Kawabata Yasunari, the president of PEN. The Japanese had every reason to be proud of the congress's success, the first major cultural event staged in Japan after the war. Even schoolchildren had contributed money to support it.

Although I was one of the least distinguished delegates, I was a favorite with Japanese newspaper reporters because I could speak Japanese. Each of them was eager to ask such penetrating questions as "What do foreign writers think of Japan?" "Who are their favorite Japanese authors?" "Is it true that the delegates, not satisfied with the Japanese banquet last night, went afterward to a restaurant for a steak?" I quickly grew tired of such questions, but the professional writers, accustomed to being interviewed, replied patiently to each reporter, never saying, "I've already answered that question ten times!"

I knew one of the reporters, Takahashi Tan, a former prisoner. Takahashi had been a Dōmei reporter on Guam where he was captured, close to starvation. I had interrogated him in Hawaii and, years later, saw him occasionally in Japan. We shared one unforgettable experience. A prisoner I interrogated in Hawaii had told me how much he missed hearing classical music. Accordingly, I decided, without obtaining authorization from anyone, to take a phonograph and records to the prisoner-of-war camp. Aware that not all the prisoners would enjoy classical music, I bought in Honolulu some records of Japanese popular music that I played first. Then I put on Beethoven's *Eroica* Symphony. The place was the camp's shower room, and the records sounded marvelous. At first as I listened to the music, I could not help but observe the expressions on the prisoners' faces. I felt that the music had created a bond between us, overriding differences in nationality and the war. But before long, I was so carried away by the music that I could not think of anything else. Even now, if asked which my favorite symphony is, I invariably answer "the *Eroica*."

After the war ended, I wrote an essay describing the concert, but the *New Yorker* turned it down. By coincidence, Takahashi wrote an article with the same title as mine, but his appeared in a Japanese magazine. In it he related that he had at first wondered why I had chosen to play the *Eroica*. Was it because I wanted to indoctrinate the prisoners with Beethoven's ideals of freedom? Or was I trying to catch the prisoners off guard while they listened to the music? In the end, however, Takahashi decided that my only intent was to share the music.

At the PEN Congress Takahashi drew me aside to ask me some questions, hoping that our old acquaintance would induce me to reveal the contents of confidential discussions among the delegates. In fact, there were hardly any such discussions, but those I knew about I gladly leaked to him.

The PEN Club Congress was my initiation into the world of writers. In Tokyo we all stayed at the (old) Imperial Hotel and had breakfast together. But the conversations over the breakfast table were disappointing. Although this was the first visit to

Japan for almost all the delegates, they seemed to have made little effort to acquaint themselves beforehand with Japanese culture and tended to mock what they could not understand. The one cultural event that impressed everyone was a performance of nō. However, no sooner had the performance ended than reporters clustered around the delegates to ask, "You were bored, weren't you?" They found it inconceivable that foreigners could appreciate an art that they themselves found tedious.

After a few days, the congress moved from Tokyo to Kyoto. Because I had lived in Kyoto for two years, I took it upon myself to guide some delegates to notable places. I remember especially a visit to Koke-dera (Moss Temple) with Stephen Spender, Angus Wilson, and Alberto Moravia. The only person I knew in Kyoto who owned a car was a priest at Shōren-in, who gladly agreed to drive us wherever we wished. The car was very small, but we (and the driver) squeezed in. At the Koke-dera, each one of us wrote a poem describing his impressions of the celebrated moss garden. I seldom met these writers in later years, but Spender's stay in Japan awakened his interest in Japanese literature, and he published in *Encounter,* the magazine he edited, my translation of Mishima's modern nō play *Hanjo.*

The PEN Congress was one factor that led to the acceptance of Japanese works as an integral part of the world's literature. Another factor, though I hesitate to mention it, was the publication of the two volumes of my anthology of Japanese literature in 1955 and 1956. Although the translations by Arthur Waley of *The Tale of Genji, The Pillow-Book of Sei Shōnagon,* and a selection of nō plays had attracted discriminating readers, most of Waley's books were printed in editions of only three thousand copies, half for England and half for America. Even those who recognized that his translations were masterpieces thought of them as isolated peaks rising from a void. The only history of Japanese literature in English was published in 1899 and was hopelessly out of date. My anthology thus served to satisfy a real need.

Now when I examine the contents of the two volumes of the anthology, I am surprised by the aptness of the works chosen for inclusion. Perhaps it was beginner's luck. I had begun studying Japanese literature only ten years earlier and still was ignorant of many major works. Even though I was helped by the translations by Waley and by friends who made new translations, the responsibility was ultimately mine. I surely would have done a better job if I had spent four or five years (instead of two) on the anthologies, but fifty years later, they still are used at universities in the West wherever Japanese literature is taught.

In 1955 I happened to read *Hanjo*, a modern nō play by Mishima Yukio, published in the literary magazine *Shinchō*. I had previously read some of Mishima's novels and had seen his plays performed, but this was my first acquaintance with the modern nō plays. I was so impressed by *Hanjo* that I decided to translate it.

The theater played an ever growing role in the friendship between Mishima and me. We had first met, symbolically it would seem, in front of the Kabuki Theater in Tokyo in November of the previous year. We got along well from the first, and he invited me to go with him to kabuki and nō. We never went to bunraku because Mishima, proud that he was born and bred in Tokyo, scorned the puppets as provincial.

One of my first letters from Mishima, which I received in New York early in 1956, expressed pleasure that my translation of *Hanjo* had been completed. It appeared in the January 1957 issue of *Encounter*. I sent the translation to Harold Strauss, who suggested that I try instead a publisher that specialized in books not intended for the general public. Then, however, after reading my translation of *Sotoba Komachi,* he changed his mind and decided to publish all five of Mishima's modern nō plays.

The first performance of *Hanjo* was in my English translation. The role of Yoshio was taken by Ivan Morris, who would soon be a colleague at Columbia University and a close friend. The performance was a success, encouraging Mishima, who seems to have hoped his modern nō would be performed abroad. Indeed, his decision to travel to New York in the summer of 1957 was inspired by the publication of the book. He wrote me in June, saying he would arrive in New York the following month and wanted above all to see plays, especially musicals, because he feared he might not understand the language in dramatic plays.

Soon after Mishima arrived, the *New York Times* sent a reporter to interview him. Strauss—in the interests of publicity for not only *Five Modern Nō* but also the translation of *The Sound of Waves,* which appeared about the same time—had informed the newspapers of Mishima's arrival. The reporter, whose articles on literary figures I had often read, proved to be a dolt. At first Mishima answered in English the usual questions—"Is this your first visit to New York?" "How long will you be here?" Then the reporter, consulting the background material he had been sent, said, "It says here you're publishing a book of plays and that you're also publishing a novel. Which are you anyway—a playwright or a novelist?" Mishima, in evident disgust, shifted to Japanese, leaving the interpreting to me. The questions became increasingly stupid, but I had no choice but to interpret.

After the interview, realizing that the reporter knew nothing about him, Mishima asked me what one had to do to become famous in New York. He was accustomed to people stopping him in the streets to ask for his autograph. He told me that once a young woman had held out a magic marker, asking him to autograph her underwear. The indifference of the reporter had thus come as a shock. I told him that even if Hemingway and

Faulkner walked arm in arm through Times Square, nobody would recognize them.

Not long after the book appeared, however, the publishers began to receive telephone calls from would-be producers of the nō plays. Delighted at this show of recognition, Mishima met all of them. He finally selected two unusually intelligent young men who had brilliant ideas about how the plays should be produced. Next a director was chosen and various actors and actresses were auditioned. Mishima, who had considerable experience in the theater in Japan, listened to each, sometimes urging that a line be delivered with more expression or with greater clarity. Several actresses, nervous because of the strain of the audition, burst into tears. The producers gently informed Mishima that in America it was not customary for the author to direct the plays.

The producers were sure that they would be able to raise the necessary funds for their production. The important thing, they said, was to make sure that there were no strings attached to the money, and so they were resolved to turn down any potential backer whose condition was that his wife appear in the plays. Tired of waiting for the money to be raised, Mishima went off to Mexico for a vacation. He expected that the plays would be in rehearsal by the time he returned, and while in Mexico he bought New York newspapers, hoping to find an announcement of his plays' opening.

The producers were not able to raise enough money, with or without strings. They decided that the problem was that the three modern nō plays they had chosen for a program were too similar in tone and therefore suggested to Mishima that he write a modern kyōgen to be performed between Aoi no ue and Sotoba Komachi. Mishima was aware of the difficulty of preserving kyōgen's humor in a modern adaptation, as it depends so heavily on exaggerated gestures and inflexions of speech. He decided nevertheless that it might be possible to make a modern version of *Hanago*, with the daimyo of the original changed into an industrialist and Tarōkaja into a butler. The Zen meditation scene could be rewritten as yoga, which then was popular in New York. Finally, knowing of my special interest in *kyōgen*, he asked me to write a modern version. He recognized that certain passages in the original, though quite normal expressions in medieval Japan, would not be tolerated in a modern play. For example, when the master threatens to kill Tarōkaja if he does not obey his command, this would not seem comic to a modern audience. Conversely, Mishima thought that the daimyo's wife threatening to beat Tarōkaja if he did not reveal why he was sitting in meditation was amusing and could be retained. Even today a woman carried away by anger might say the same.

Mishima gave me various other tips, but I was unable, even with great effort, to do what he always did so easily. I tried everything, even making it a comedy in the manner of Molière and giving the characters Greek names. Nothing worked. I confessed my failure to Mishima, who thereupon bought a notebook of the kind American junior high school students use and wrote a modern *kyōgen*,  based not on *Hanago* but *Busu*. He dashed off the manuscript at full speed, changing hardly a word.

The producers attempted to find backers for the new combination of two modern nō and a modern *kyōgen*, but they still had no success. This time they decided that the problem was that Americans did not like one-act plays, so they asked Mishima to rewrite three of his modern nō plays as a single play. I thought that this would be virtually impossible, even for Mishima, as the plays have entirely different characters and atmospheres. How could he join them into a single entity? But Mishima was so desirous of seeing the plays performed in New York that he did the impossible: he made one play out of the three plays. And he gave the new play an English title with a double meaning: *Long After Love*.

This heroic action did not bring any rewards. The young producers still could not find a backer. In the meantime, Mishima was running out of money. He moved from a comfortable hotel near the Waldorf Astoria to a decidedly less agreeable hotel in Greenwich Village. Worst of all, there was nothing for him to do. He told me he could not write Japanese when surrounded by people speaking other languages. He saw all the musicals on Broadway and even attended theaters where amateurs performed.

Although I was aware of his impatience, there was little I could do. I had a heavy burden of teaching, and I also lacked the money to take Mishima to the kinds of restaurants he took me to in Tokyo. So I waited and did nothing to help him. I later regretted my ineffectuality. In the end, angry with New York, Mishima left for Europe on New Year's Eve, seemingly resolved never to return.

During the late 1950s my life fell into a regular pattern. From September until the end of May each year I taught Japanese language and literature in New York at Columbia University, and then I spent the three months of the long summer vacations in Kyoto.

In those days it did not cost any more to make stops on the way to one's final destination, so I usually spent some time in San Francisco and Honolulu going to and from Japan. Occasionally the plane refueled at Wake Island, and the passengers, irrespective of class, would sit in a waiting room until the plane was ready. On one occasion I found myself next to Japan's foreign minister, Fujiwara Aiichirō, and had my first conversation with a senior member of the Japanese government.

Later on, I took a direct flight from New York to Tokyo by way of Anchorage in Alaska. Memories of the dismal Aleutian Islands were still so vivid that I was never tempted to stop off in Alaska, but the Anchorage airport was rather interesting. Apart from an immense stuffed polar bear, it offered Eskimo wood carvings and a view of distant mountains. The Japanese passengers, starved for *soba* (buckwheat noodles), customarily gulped down a bowl or two while waiting for the plane to leave. At the tax-free shop, the American sales personnel cried "Irasshaimase!" to whoever entered, regardless of facial features, assuming that anyone who wished to buy a present must be Japanese.

Each year it was a delight to arrive in Japan after eight or nine months in New York. After disembarking at Haneda, I would search for friends in the crowd meeting the plane, sure that several would be there, even very busy people. Haneda was close enough to the city to permit the traditional Japanese welcome. Although I would be sleepy after a night on the plane, I was eager to hear my friends' news. I then would be taken to the room reserved for me at the Akasaka Prince Hotel. The hotel, formerly the residence of the Korean royal family, had a charm no modern hotel possesses, and the service was superb. There was a button in each room that, when pressed, lit a light in the corridor, and within thirty seconds a man would knock at the door, ready to wrap a parcel, polish one's shoes, or send a telegram. The room was cleaned each morning while I was at breakfast in the dining room. Whoever cleaned the room somehow knew exactly when I left.

After a few days in Tokyo I returned to Kyoto, where I was delighted to see Nagai-san and Okumura-san and to set foot once again in "my" house. Pusuke, the Okumuras' dog, greeted me effusively. One year when I arrived in Kyoto, I found that it was too cool for the summer clothes I had brought from New York, and Nagai-san lent me a suit. Somehow it made me happy to discover that we were the same size. That was true of our shoes as well.

For three or four years my main occupation during the summers in Kyoto was translating the plays of Chikamatsu Monzaemon. Kyoto summers are justly famed for their heat, and Japanese friends thought I was crazy to live there voluntarily, but Imakumano was relatively cool, and for me, being in Kyoto was more important than the heat.

Translating Chikamatsu was a great test of my command of Japanese. I had resolved to translate every word of the original texts, even in the parts of the plays like the *michiyuki* (travel scene) that usually were omitted by Japanese translators, who dismissed the poetry of these scenes as mere ornamentation. Probably my most important discovery as a Chikamatsu scholar was the dramatic importance of the *michiyuki*. During the course of the journey, Tokubei or Jihei (or whoever the hero might be) develops from a weakling into a man capable of killing his beloved and himself. I wrote that he became taller as he walked.

I had help from Professor Mori Shū of Osaka Municipal University, who came to Kyoto every week, despite the heat, carrying every commentated edition of the play I was translating. He would spread the books open on a table and read each commentator's interpretation of difficult passages before he ventured his own opinion, always in extremely polite language. We sometimes read only a few lines during an afternoon.

Even when I felt satisfied that I had fully understood a passage, there was the problem of finding English words that not only accurately conveyed the sense of the original but were natural and also easy for actors to pronounce. Despite my resolve to translate every word, I had no choice but to omit most of the puns because they usually required long explanations and were not effective in translation. I tried, however, to find equivalents for the *engo* (related words) that Chikamatsu so frequently employed. Here is how I rendered part of the song of Tahei, the comic villain in *The Love Suicides at Amijima*:

Jihei the paper dealer—
Too much love for Koharu
Has made him a foolscap.
He wastepapers sheets of gold
Till his fortune's shredded to confetti
And Jihei himself is like scrap paper
You can't even blow your nose on!

In this passage different words relating to paper (because Jihei sells paper) are used for humorous effect. I had always supposed that *engo* were unique to Japan, but by chance while I was making this translation I read a book about the coming of the New Deal under President Franklin Roosevelt. I was surprised to find *engo* in sentences like "The airlines introduced a crash program." Of course, the *engo* was accidental! The author had subconsciously chosen related synonyms—"crash program" rather than "emergency program"—because of the connection between airlines and crashes. Perhaps this occurs in all writing, but Chikamatsu elevated an unconscious habit into an art.

In the years following my translation of eleven of Chikamatsu's plays, I translated both nō and modern works. Some were performed abroad, probably the most successful being Mishima's *Sado kōshaku fujin* (*Madame de Sade*). A Swedish company's version, directed by Ingmar Bergman, was a great success in New York, though most in the audience, unable to understand Swedish, listened to my translation through headphones.

Most translators stay away from plays. Some believe that reading a play can never be a substitute for seeing it performed, and others know that translated plays rarely sell as well as fiction.

My persistence in making translations probably stems from a love of the theater that goes back to childhood.

When my translations are performed on the stage or on the radio, I sometimes wince at phrases that sound stilted, even though I always read my translations aloud before publishing them. Sometimes my English is "infected" by the original Japanese text. For instance, when faced with the Japanese words *ame ga futte iru*, a translator is apt to write without thinking, "The rain is falling." Although it is grammatically correct, nobody says this in English. Rather, we say, "It is raining."

Any work of Japanese literature is likely to have traps for the unwary translator. These are particularly dangerous in plays, when a badly chosen expression may make a scene ridiculous. Sometimes, however, inadequacy in a translation cannot be helped. When I saw a French production of *Madame de Sade*, I realized how closely Mishima had observed the conventions of the French stage in this play. No English translation could match a French translation in naturalness. But despite all obstacles, if the translator really admires a play, he will persist, hoping somehow to capture what he knows is in the original.

In 1961, my seventh year since I began teaching at Columbia, I had a sabbatical leave of one year. Nowadays, American professors feel free to abandon their teaching for a year or two whenever it suits their convenience, but in those days the seventh year, like Sunday at the end of a week, brought a long-awaited freedom from teaching. I was fortunate to obtain a grant from a foundation to do research on traditional forms of Japanese drama. It seemed, in prospect, a wonderful year.

If I had been given this opportunity a few years earlier, I certainly would have spent the year in Kyoto in "my" little house, but a new tunnel for the Shinkansen (bullet train) was being constructed nearby and the valley in front of the house had been filled with the excavated dirt and stones, destroying the view. So I searched for another place to live in Kyoto, but none was remotely comparable to the house I had so much enjoyed. I thus decided to make a fresh start in Tokyo, justifying this decision in terms of the greater variety of theater available in the capital.

The apartment I rented was in Harajuku, then a quiet enclave between Shibuya and Shinjuku, whose most conspicuous buildings were churches and antique shops. The apartment was rather bleak, especially after Kyoto, but the greatest inconvenience was not having anyone to cook for me. I either cooked for myself or bought sushi in the neighborhood.

After an initial flurry of invitations to dinner from friends welcoming me to Tokyo, I generally ate alone, for the first time in Japan. In the past when I had made brief visits to Tokyo, friends hurried to make dinner engagements with me, but when they learned I would be in Tokyo for a whole year, they felt no need to hurry.

When I met Mishima Yukio soon after my arrival, he said that if I didn't mind eating simple food, I should feel free to have dinner at his house whenever I had nowhere else to go. I was grateful for the invitation, and it would have given me pleasure to have dinner with him, but I could not bring myself to telephone and confess that I had nowhere else to go.

At this point another friend, Yoshida Ken'ichi, somehow guessing I might be lonely, invited me to have dinner on Thursday nights with him and his friends. I had met Yoshida during my second year in Japan, when I was staying at the house of

Shimanaka Hōji, who lived not far from Yoshida. Yoshida was the only Japanese friend with whom I normally spoke English. Nagai-san was completely fluent in English, but he seemed more himself when he spoke Japanese. Yoshida's English, however, was so exactly that of an upper-class Englishman that it seemed odd to speak Japanese with him, though we did when other Japanese were present. Yoshida had been favorably impressed by my little book *Japanese Literature*, based on five lectures given in Cambridge, and translated it so well that the Japanese version has sold many more copies than the original.

Thursday nights became the highlight of my week. Generally we were joined by Kawakami Tetsutarō and Ishikawa Jun, who shared Yoshida's love of saké. We would meet at the bar Sophia. From there we went on to Hachimaki Okada for dinner and  sometimes from there to another place for drinking. Although Yoshida published several books about Japanese cuisine, he rarely ate anything except when his wife was present. Instead, he would look lovingly at the food rather as if he were admiring a beautiful painting that he certainly did not wish to deface. But he made up for not eating by the quantity of liquor he drank. Although he was fond of every kind of alcoholic beverage, he especially loved saké and once described a saké from Niigata as "liquid moonlight." When he was drunk he babbled happily, sometimes in English, sometimes in Japanese, and equally unintelligibly in both.

In return for Yoshida's kindness, I thought I would translate one of his essays, but it proved extremely difficult. He could have written the essay in flawless English if he had so chosen, but because he was writing in Japanese, he wanted the style to be as Japanese as possible, even if this interfered with easy comprehension. Despairing of coming up with a translation that would satisfy him, I never attempted to publish it.

I later had lengthy dialogues with both
Kawakami and Ishikawa. Before I talked with
Kawakami, I asked that as a special favor, we
not drink during our discussion. I thought he
had agreed, but before I knew it, whiskey appeared. The dialogue was nonetheless successful; at any rate, I learned much about Japanese
literature from this distinguished critic.

The dialogue with Ishikawa, by contrast, was painful. Although he spoke in a benevolent manner, he pointed out error
after error in my account of Tokugawa literature, being able to
do this because of his extraordinary knowledge of that period.
Several times he asked in kindly tones, "Why didn't you show
this to me before publishing it?" But I could not imagine under
what circumstances I would have been so bold as to send my
manuscript to a man known not only for his novels and essays
but also for his extremely high standards. Despite my shock, I
believe that Ishikawa liked me, and I certainly admired him. I
was the first to translate (in 1961) one of his works, the novella
Asters.

When I mentioned to a friend my disappointment in the
dialogue, he said that Ishikawa would not have consented to
talk with me if he did not respect my work. At first I could not
accept these words of consolation, fearing that Ishikawa had
contempt for what I had written; but then I reminded myself
how extraordinarily lucky I was to spend Thursday nights with
such men as Yoshida, Kawakami, and Ishikawa, who took me
into their conversations despite the considerable difference in
age and knowledge. Indeed, Ishikawa had criticized my work as
he would the work of a Japanese, without making concessions
because I was a foreigner.

Yoshida, Kawakami, and Ishikawa were *bunjin* (men of letters),
a class that was gradually disappearing. They shared nostalgia for
Tokyo when the city was crisscrossed with rivers and canals and

there were trees everywhere, and they delighted in remnants of the old culture. They also were generous, even extravagant, with their money, in the manner traditional in Edo. On one occasion when we went to a hotel for drinks, Yoshida ordered champagne and caviar. A band was playing. When the music stopped, Yoshida summoned the leader and, pressing a thousand-yen note into his hand, asked for a favorite piece of music. The piece was played, and Yoshida asked a second time, again pressing a thousand-yen note into the man's hand. The third time, Yoshida again proffered the banknote, saying, "Anything at all!" (*Nandemo ii ya*). A thousand yen then was a fairly large amount of money, and Yoshida was by no means affluent, but he took pleasure in being a *bunjin*.

Sometimes others joined us for dinner, younger men whose exceptional talents had been recognized by Yoshida and the others. This is how I met Shinoda Hajime. Shinoda, a very heavy man who once had been a judo champion, did not look in the least like a scholar of literature, but he was in fact extraordinarily well versed not only in English literature (which he taught) but in the languages and literatures of half a dozen other European countries. He was even more deeply moved by the classics of Chinese and Japanese literature, and one of his last books was on the medieval poet Shinkei. He was equally familiar with music, including difficult modern compositions that I have never enjoyed. The first time we ate at Hachimaki Okada, after examining the menu, Shinoda ordered *everything*. When I teased him about this later on, he explained that the portions were very small.

On one occasion (after we had been drinking) Shinoda, Yoshida, and I got into a taxi. The taxi proceeded for about ten minutes then, in the middle of nowhere, Yoshida suddenly shouted, "*Tomare!*" (Stop!) The driver stopped the car and Yoshida unsteadily got out, whereupon Shinoda picked him up in his arms and deposited him back in the car. This happened two or three more times. In extremely high spirits throughout, Yoshida obviously enjoyed a game worthy of an eighteenth-century *bunjin*.

27

During my sabbatical leave in Tokyo in 1961, I spent much of my time reading about and going to the Japanese theater. My studies resulted in two books, one on bunraku (1965) and the other on nō (1966). These books, the most beautiful I have published, were honored with introductions by Tanizaki Jun'ichirō and Ishikawa Jun, respectively.

My most important collaborator was the photographer Kaneko Keizō. Accounts of bunraku that I had read inevitably claimed that while watching a performance, the audience forgets the operators and sees only the puppets. But in photographs of bunraku, the operators in their bright costumes are more conspicuous than the puppets. In an actual performance, one has the time to forget the operators, but a photograph catches only a particular instant and there is no time to forget. Kaneko, however, had made a discovery. In a  performance, the operators are momentarily concealed by the puppets, thereby creating the illusion that the puppets are moving independently. Kaneko sought out these moments, and his photographs were magically effective.

The bunraku book benefited from the brilliant layouts by the paper-cut artist Miyata Masayuki, and each copy contained a recording of a passage from a play sung by the chanter Takemoto Tsunadayū. Yoshida Ken'ichi provided the Japanese translation. No book has been more fortunate in its collaborators.

Although photographing bunraku is difficult, in some ways nō is even more difficult. Whereas a performance of bunraku is likely to be repeated many times a month, a nō play usually is performed by a particular actor only once. Accordingly, I remember that on one occasion Kaneko braved a high fever to take pictures of a performance of nō that I wished to include in my book because he knew he would not have another chance.

In addition to attending performances of nō, I decided to take lessons in singing. Torigoe Bunzō, who later became the director of the Waseda Theater Museum, joined me in lessons with Sakurama Michio, an outstanding actor of the Konparu school. During the first lesson Sakurama-san described the characteristics of this school. One feature is to open the mouth wide when singing or declaiming, but not to show the teeth. I tried to follow this prescription but had trouble pronouncing anything more complicated than ba-ba-ba. Nō certainly was more difficult than *kyōgen*, but at least it provided printed texts.

The first play I studied was *Hashi Benkei*, no doubt chosen because it is easy to sing and has an uncomplicated plot. I enjoyed the lessons, but I kept wishing I was learning a play of greater literary interest. One day I asked Sakurama-san whether we might next study a play I liked better. He asked which one, and I answered, "*Yuya.*" He gave a great laugh and said this was like going from kindergarten to the university with nothing in between, but in the end, considering that my stay in Japan was limited, he agreed to teach us *Yuya*.

I first became interested in *Yuya*, a play I had not seen performed, because of Mishima Yukio's enthusiasm. He told me that the character Taira no Munemori intrigued him because of his resemblance to a Renaissance tyrant. Munemori's heart is set on seeing the cherry blossoms at Kiyomizu with his mistress Yuya, and he refuses to permit her to leave him even when she reads a letter from her dying mother. Mishima added that some actors thought Yuya's real reason for wanting to return home was not to see her dying mother but to be with a lover. In Mishima's modern nō *Yuya*, the climactic scene is the arrival of Yuya's "dying" mother from the country. She is brimming with health and vulgar good spirits.

Just at this time I began to receive letters from my own mother saying that she was not well and asking me to return soon. It was almost too exact a parallel with *Yuya*. It was hard to know how to evaluate the letter. My mother had a highly strung temperament, and sometimes when I failed to write or telephone her for a few weeks, she would send a note to the effect that if I ever got around to communicating with her, I would probably discover that she was dead. But when she was really ill (as had happened a few times), she would pretend she was suffering from nothing worse than a cold. Thinking that her letters probably meant no more than that she was lonely, I promised to return in February and not in September, as I had planned. My mother seemed satisfied with this promise.

About the same time, I had a letter from Arthur Waley saying that he had broken his right arm. On top of this misfortune, the University of London was about to drive him from his house because it had decided to install a computer (then an extremely large machine) on the premises. Worst of all, his companion, Beryl de Zoete, with whom he had lived for thirty years, was dying of Huntington's disease. I decided I would go first to London to comfort Waley and from there to my mother in New York. I did not realize that I was following the pattern described in another work of Japanese literature: Natsume Sōseki's *Kokoro*.

I left Japan in December and went to Europe by way of Southeast Asia, stopping at places I had long wanted to see. It is hard for me now to recall why I did not proceed at once to London and New York. I suppose I thought that this was my last chance to see Southeast Asia and that a few days' delay would not matter. I was wrong on both counts.

I arrived in London from Japan on a cold gray morning. I climbed the stairs to Waley's apartment thinking that they must be a strain on a man of his age. He met me without a display of emotion but suggested that we go at once to the floor above where Beryl de Zoete lay dying. I had known her for some years and was aware that she suffered from Huntington's disease, a terrible condition that causes sufferers to keep incessantly moving their hands and other parts of their body. He said, "Don't ask her any questions. She understands and will try to answer. Just say you are glad to see her and kiss her." But when I saw Beryl, she was so ravaged by illness that I could not kiss her. Waley had brought her home from the hospital because the stupid nurses, not realizing that Beryl's mind was unaffected despite her affliction, treated her as a thing. Waley spent his days looking after her.

We went downstairs in silence. Waley opened up a tin of steak and kidneys and warmed it up for our lunch. He had written me that he probably would never be able to write again.

That was why I was in London. Desperately wishing to comfort him, I offered to become his secretary and write down whatever he dictated, but he shook off the suggestion. He said that he intended to spend his remaining years reading European literature and that he had given up his oriental studies. I was totally unable to bring him comfort. This was our last meeting. I wrote him several times afterward, but there was no reply.

I left London for New York the day after visiting Waley. In the plane my thoughts kept returning to the sick room where Beryl lay dying. Perhaps I was now on the point of confronting a similar scene that was even more painful. Although I had felt sure that my mother's illness was due mainly to loneliness, I began to doubt my conviction. I was desperately eager to reach New York as soon as possible, but as my bad luck would have it, there was a storm in New York and the plane was diverted to Montreal.

On arrival, the passengers were directed to a waiting room. The sound of the piped-in music got on my nerves so badly that I asked if there was nowhere in the airport free of music, but there was none. Eventually we were informed that the plane would not leave until the following morning. I passed a sleepless night in a hotel.

28

The plane left Montreal for New York the next morning. As soon as I arrived, I telephoned an aunt to learn in which hospital my mother was, and I went directly there. My mother did not recognize me. Although she occasionally said a word or two, I could not understand what, if anything, she was trying to communicate. My aunt told me, "If you had only come yesterday, you could have talked with her." I recalled then the delay of the plane, the wait in the airport, and the music I had been unable to escape.

My mother died the same day. Afterward, I went back to my apartment, tormented by the conviction that I had been a bad son. Why had I not hurried back to New York as soon as she wrote me that she was not feeling well? I could not help asking myself this question again and again.

That night I had a telephone call from Tokyo. Shimanaka Hōji called to inform me that I had won the Kikuchi Kan Prize.

He asked whether I would return to Japan to accept it. Although I did not weep when my mother died and I did not weep now, I felt torn between misery and joy.

The funeral was, inevitably, wrenching. I took a last look at my mother's face, but it had been cosmetically beautified, all the wrinkles removed. She was hardly recognizable. People tried to console me, but because I could not weep they must have thought me heartless. I was unable to say anything to people who kindly attempted to cheer me. I made up my mind to return to Japan and left immediately after the funeral. While the plane was crossing the American continent, I was in such a daze that I have no recollection now of what (if anything) I did during the six or seven hours. The plane, which went from New York to Tokyo without any change, stopped in Honolulu. Two old friends whom I had alerted to my brief visit came to meet the plane and comfort me. At first I was so distraught that I did not even recognize them, but the affection they showed during the few minutes we spent together helped dissolve my self-centered grief.

I arrived in Tokyo just in time to attend the lunch given by Ambassador Edwin Reischauer in my honor. I had known him during my year at Harvard and had admired him not only as a teacher and scholar but also as a friend. Accordingly, I was delighted when, at the outset of President John F. Kennedy's administration, he was appointed as the American ambassador to Japan; he knew the language well and was exceptionally familiar with Japanese history and culture. There could not have been a better ambassador at a time when relations between Japan and the United States had deteriorated because of the war in Vietnam. Reischauer was still recovering from the effects of a wound inflicted by a madman and had to use a cane when he walked, but he remained cheerful, though (as I later learned) the wound and the transfusion of tainted blood continued to give him pain for the rest of his life.

The ambassador had invited to the lunch Sasaki Mosaku, Ikejima Shimpei, and other editors of *Bungei shunjū*, which awarded the Kikuchi Kan Prize, and also some of my closest friends—Shimanaka Hōji, Mishima Yukio, and Yoshida Ken'ichi. (Nagai Michio was in Hong Kong.) Not only was I happy they had come, but seeing them made me feel as if I had come back to life. The photograph taken that day on the steps of the embassy (which I was visiting for the first time) shows the ambassador, Mrs. Reischauer and the guests, and me. I am smiling, though when I first set out on my journey from New York to Tokyo, I thought I would never smile again.

At the ceremony where I received the prize, I naturally expressed my gratitude and my awareness of what an honor it was to receive so distinguished an award. But even as I spoke, I could not help but think of Arthur Waley, whom I had seen a week earlier under the unhappy circumstances I have related. I wished I could somehow share the prize with him, but I said merely that I felt as if I were accepting for him too, though he deserved the prize far more than I did. Without the example of Waley's marvelous translations to inspire me, I doubt that I would have devoted my life to transmitting to the world the beauty of Japanese literature.

At the party following the ceremony, I met other old friends, each one precious to me. Of course, my joy at seeing them did not make me forget the loss I had suffered, but I was strongly aware of how fortunate I was to have such friends. A few days later I joined the usual group at Hachimaki Okada. Ishikawa-san, remembering that my mother's illness had prevented me from joining the others in their annual expedition to Niigata to sample the new saké, asked me about *gokendō*. I did not recognize the term, but someone explained it was a polite word for another person's mother. Then there flashed into my head the passage in *Nozarashi kikō* (*Skeleton in the Fields*, which I had translated) where Bashō wrote, "The daylilies in the northern room had been withered by frost, and there was no trace of them now." Bashō's grief for his mother, who had died in his absence, was expressed in terms of a plant that had withered and disappeared, not leaving a trace. The allusion to ancient Chinese literature exactly communicated Bashō's feelings. I sometimes have quoted Bashō for the same reason.

I went again to Kyoto and spent a night in my old house. Although the building of the Shinkansen had destroyed the beauty of the scenery, the house itself was still lovely and everything in it was familiar. The old clock on the wall was still ticking, and I remembered without even thinking the location of every light switch. This little house, where I had lived happily while I was first discovering what life in Japan was like, was my home, more than any other house in which I have lived. Every corner was not only familiar but full of memories.

I visited the Chishaku-in, where I had studied calligraphy years before and had my picture taken together with my friend Nishizaki Shōmyō, a priest of the temple, seated in front of the magnificent *fusuma-e* (screen paintings). I went to the Kitano Tenmangū, where the plum blossoms were first opening. Although I knew from many poems how much the fragrance of plum blossoms was appreciated by innumerable generations of Japanese, I had never really been aware of any special fragrance

even when I stood directly under a plum tree in bloom. Obviously, my sense of smell was deficient. This time, in order to savor fully the most typical fragrance of Japan, I pressed my head against the blossoms, as a photograph taken at the time reveals. Only then did I manage to catch a whiff of the celebrated scent. I suppose that people who have grown up in the

West think of the scent of flowers in terms of the strong perfume of the rose or the carnation, and it takes some effort to
catch the delicate fragrance of plum blossoms, but it was natural for the Japanese to praise this elusive fragrance rather than
the heavy scent of the lily. The Japanese of the past (and probably of the present too) found strong fragrances cloying and
prized instead the clean but almost imperceptible perfume of
plum blossoms, just as they preferred faint coloring to bright
primary colors in paintings or avoided strong flavors in Japanese cuisine. This moment of recognition brought pleasure. Indeed, every experience during my short stay in Japan gave me
pleasure and contributed to my recovery.

By the time I returned to New York, I had become a human
being again. But I had not shed my feelings of guilt entirely, and
as a kind of penance, I decided not to spend the summer in Japan, my usual practice. Of course I knew that penance could not
bring my mother back, and I suspected that my feelings of guilt
would last a long time and that they were likely to be accompanied by attacks of depression, but I now knew that whenever I
struck bottom I could depend on Japan and the Japanese to help
me rise again.

29

In January 1964 the International Congress of Orientalists
was held in New Delhi. I had visited India several times since
my first visit in 1953 because it cost only slightly more for a
round-the-world airplane ticket than for a round-trip ticket
from New York to Tokyo. Sometimes I went to Tokyo by way of
India mainly in order to buy gifts for friends in Japan. In part I
decided to attend the congress because New Delhi would be
pleasantly cool in January, and in part because I would be able

to spend a week in Japan on my way back from India to New York. Unfortunately, while in Europe on the way to India, I developed an intestinal problem. Even a healthy person is likely to have a bout of diarrhea while in India, but I was sick even before I arrived.

I managed to survive by eating only bread and honey. This became monotonous, but I hesitated to eat anything more exciting. Even after reaching Tokyo I was still in poor shape, but I had promised Chūō kōron sha to take part in a lecture tour together with Itō Sei, Hirabayashi Taiko, and Ōe Kenzaburō. Learning of my illness, Itō-san kindly gave me a medicine called Seirogan, originally invented during the Russo-Japanese War, which looked and tasted like charcoal. It worked, and I was soon feeling much better.

More important, I had my first meeting with Ōe-san. For a time on the train to Nagoya we sat facing each other without speaking, he perusing a copy of *Esquire* while I dutifully read a periodical devoted to Japanese literature. It did not take long for this "confrontation" to end with one laugh from Ōe. His sense of humor resembled my own.

Although at that time I had not read anything by Ōe, soon afterward I read *A Private Matter*. I was so excited that I sent a telegram to Barney Rosset, the president of Grove Press (which had published my anthologies of Japanese literature), urging him to obtain the rights to publish a translation. When a good translation appeared, it led to friendship between Ōe and Rosset.

From this time on, meeting Ōe was one of the pleasures of being in Japan. We ate together and drank together, sometimes getting quite drunk. On one memorable occasion when he invited me to his house, he prepared oxtail stew, his culinary specialty. We listened together to recordings of operas, especially those sung by Maria Callas, as he shared my enthusiasm for her voice. Indeed, after her death, he wrote a moving article about Callas that he dedicated to me.

It became my custom to bring him from New York some operatic recordings not yet available in Japan. But one year when I telephoned, expecting to offer him the usual gift, he seemed reluctant to set a date for a meeting. We did not meet even once that year. I naturally was puzzled and hurt and tried in vain to think of something I might have done to annoy him. If we met by accident at a large gathering, I would ask why he was unwilling to meet me. He gave various answers. One time he said he was reading William Blake and would get in touch with me when he finished his reading. But Blake had nothing to do with me, and he did not get in touch. I wanted badly to restore our friendship, but I never found out what caused his coldness.

I asked friends who knew Ōe to help find out the reasons for the change in his attitude. One friend brought the news that it was because Ōe, being accustomed to drink with me, had given up drinking and therefore we could not dine together. Another said Ōe was annoyed because I had not translated his books.

I resigned myself regretfully to never learning why he had become distant. Sometimes, however, he surprised me with his kindness. When, for example, I received the Inoue Yasushi Prize, he gave a talk in my honor, even though he originally had not planned to attend the ceremony, which took place at a highly inconvenient time for him. On another occasion he flattered me by saying that I should write not only about Japanese literature but about the literatures of the whole world. But if I supposed that such gestures of kindness signified that our relationship was to be restored, I was mistaken. Twice when we were chosen by organizations that wished to give an award to one Japanese and one non-Japanese, he refused, apparently unwilling to be associated with me.

It was thanks to Ōe, however, that I first became friendly with Abe Kōbō, who became, after Mishima's death, my closest friend in the literary world. I had met Abe in New York in the autumn of 1964 when his novel *Woman in the Dunes* was published there.

He, Teshigahara Hiroshi (the director of the celebrated film made from the novel), and a young woman, their interpreter, visited my office at Columbia. I was annoyed by the inference that I needed an interpreter and paid no attention to the young woman. Only years later did I learn she was Ono Yōko.

I evidently produced a bad impression on Abe. I was suffering from jet lag at the time, but Abe (a graduate in medicine) concluded that my somnolence was due to drug addiction. Later, when the three of us were in Japan, Ōe suggested that we have dinner together, but Abe refused. Finally, however, he yielded and from then on we often ate together. The year they shared the Tanizaki Prize (Abe with *Friends* and Ōe with *The Silent Cry*), nobody was happier than I. But then, while in New York, I learned that they had quarreled. I childishly hoped that my presence in Japan would bring them together again, but this did not happen.

Abe's novels were sometimes criticized for their seeming impersonality and lack of overt human feelings, but this was a mistaken judgment. I always felt something exceptionally warm in Abe, though perhaps I did not know enough to understand this complicated man completely. His many facets included a grasp of science and mathematics that I have never possessed. But even without being a novelist, it was easy to admire his devotion to his craft that made him rewrite each of his novels many times, thereby severely limiting their number. His devotion to the theater, though it came rather late in life, was equally strong. He spent countless hours painstakingly directing the actors of his plays according to a system he himself had invented.

I was no less impressed by Abe's political honesty. Although he had been a member of the Japan Communist Party and to the end believed in some of its ideals, his experiences in Eastern Europe compelled him to recognize that whenever the Communist Party took political power, its ideals were inevitably per-

verted. Other writers of leftist convictions who went to the
Soviet Union were flattered by the special treatment they received as guests of the regime and hesitated to express what
doubts they felt, but even though Abe's disappointment was
profound, he could not remain silent.

Abe became persona non grata in the Soviet Union. When his
Russian translator went to Japan, she was ordered not to meet
him, though she was permitted to meet me. One day the translator and I went for a walk, and at a prearranged place Abe's car
rolled up, quite by accident, and Abe and the translator had a re-
union. She was one of those who had helped Abe achieve his
awakening.

But I should not give the impression that whenever Abe and I
met, we engaged in serious political or artistic discussion. Most
of our time together was spent in laughter. We shared a love of
paradox, and he had an agreeably wicked tongue when discussing
the works of writers he did not like. He often drove from Hakone,
where he wrote, to Usami where I have an apartment. Over an immense plate of sashimi at a local restaurant, Abe would delight
me with his observations. For my part, I would amuse Abe by my
total ignorance of even the most basic scientific facts.

I was lucky to have known two such men as Ōe and Abe.
Even though my relationship with Ōe turned into an enigma, I
still have many happy memories of this extraordinary writer.

30

It was probably in 1964 that I made up my mind to write a
history of Japanese literature. As far back as 1953, while teaching
at Cambridge, I had written a review expressing my dissatisfaction with the existing histories of Japanese literature, by both

Japanese and foreigners. I did not mean to imply in the review that I could write a better history, as I probably was well aware of my deficiencies as a scholar of Japanese literature.

At Cambridge I had read works of classical Japanese literature with my students. I also had taught Japanese history up to the Meiji Restoration. But not until I returned to Columbia did I give a course covering Japanese literature from the ancient history *Kojiki* to works by living authors. I tried to make the course as personal and as interesting as possible. Remembering my boredom when other professors had read manuscripts prepared many years earlier, I spoke without notes, relying not on dates or on lists of members of a "school" of poetry or fiction but on my personal reactions to the works I was discussing. I tried to communicate what I found significant in each work.

My students were expected to read existing translations of major works and the two volumes of my anthology of Japanese literature, which provided a framework for my teaching. I enjoyed

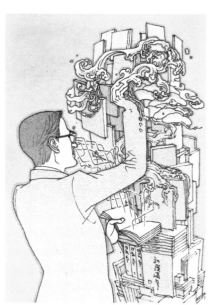

teaching this course and tried to make it different each year. Later I sometimes got letters from students telling me that although they had forgotten what I had taught them about Japanese literature, they remembered the enthusiasm revealed in my lectures.

As I went on reading Japanese literature, I gradually filled in the holes in my knowledge. It occurred to me at some point that I might write down my lectures, not for use with my own class but in the hopes that people elsewhere might find them informative. I began to type a manuscript roughly based on my teaching, not bothering to look up dates or anything else I did not know, delaying this until a later rewriting. In a short time I had written about 250 pages and had already reached the thirteenth century. I thought it would take no more than two years to complete the history.

About this time I read that Japanese airlines were now permitted to fly from Tokyo to Moscow. I suddenly felt like seeing the Soviet Union, a mysterious country that so often seemed to threaten the peace of the rest of the world. Not knowing anyone there, I asked Abe Kōbō, who had visited the Soviet Union, if he could introduce anyone. He wrote down the name and address of his translator, Irina Lwowa.

The flight over Siberia was memorable, not only because of the scenery, but also because of its literary associations, especially the dread of exile in this desolate region. When I reached Moscow, an Intourist officer told me that a room had been assigned to me in the National Hotel. There was no question of choice.

The next day I managed to make my way to the address Abe had given me. Finally, I found the apartment and rang the bell. There was no answer. I rang twice more, but still no answer, whereupon I tore a page from my notebook and, leaning on a wall, started writing a message in Japanese. As I wrote, the door opened. Professor Lwowa's husband, seeing me through the peephole in the door, had concluded from my writing Japanese that I was not to be feared. He let me in and told me that Professor Lwowa was in Leningrad. He spoke Japanese; in fact, Japanese was virtually the only language I spoke while in the Soviet Union.

After a few days of sightseeing in Moscow, thrilled by the sight of the Kremlin and the fairy-tale domes of St. Basil's Church, I went on to Leningrad where I met Professor Lwowa. I liked her immediately, and I think the feeling was mutual. We had a great deal to talk about, probably because we shared the experience of having studied Japanese literature, but also because we had hitherto been prevented by the unfriendly relations between our

two countries from enjoying any form of communication. Our conversations took place for the most part while we walked, making it less likely we could be overheard. When we boarded a bus, she murmured to me, "From now on, silence."

Our conversations were in no sense political, but she spoke with surprising frankness, considering that she hardly knew me. When I praised the lovely architecture of Leningrad, she pointed to one building and said, "In each room of that house, a whole family now lives. The rooms were cut up into such small units that in one apartment the painting on the ceiling may show only one foot of an allegorical figure, the other foot being in the next apartment." I was amused but also strangely moved to think of the dreary lives led in once magnificent rooms. When I praised the architecture and statues in the Moscow subway stations, she said with a smile that at the time these splendid stations were built, many thousands of people had nowhere to sleep.

I learned intuitively during my brief stay in the Soviet Union to praise everything I saw. I guessed that if I were to criticize anything, this would probably evoke patriotic sentiments of less interest than the candid reactions to my praise.

I met Professor Evgenia Pinus, the professor of Japanese at the University of Leningrad. Although she spoke Japanese well, she told me that she had been allowed to go to Japan only once, as an interpreter for a delegation. One day they went to the Kabuki Theater, but after half an hour the delegation had had enough, and she had to leave with them, even though it had been her dream to see kabuki. She said, "But I had two hours of free time when I could wander as I pleased in Tokyo."

Two hours! I had spent not two hours but four or five years in Japan. I felt a kind of guilt that things had been too easy for me, too hard for her. She uttered not one word of complaint, but my heart went out to her.

We talked about the history I was writing. I told her of my plan to write an enjoyable book that would reveal the beauty of Japanese literature. I added, "I don't intend to include dates or other biographical information. I want to concentrate on the works themselves." She asked, "But what if readers need to know the dates?" I replied, "They can find them in other books." She asked, "Which books?" I realized that there were no others, in English at any rate.

That is how I came to change the entire conception of my history. I realized that I would have to include even information that bored me. I could make my interpretations and evaluations as personal as I wished, but I also would have to supply the basic facts. As a result of this decision, it took me not two years but twenty-five years to complete the history. This, though I did not realize it at the time, was the greatest benefit I received from my visit to the Soviet Union.

When the Intourist car called at my hotel to take me to the airport, I was seen off by Professor Pinus and two of her students. We exchanged in Japanese the customary greetings, apologies, and expressions of gratitude. After this ceremony, I saw for the first time that there was another passenger in the car, a Japanese who no doubt had heard these polite phrases. Surely he must have wondered why four Russians should have spoken Japanese, but he did not say a word all the way to the airport.

It took a long time to go through the formalities of leaving the Soviet Union. Even once aboard the plane, I felt tension, as I had heard of Soviet citizens who for some reason were removed from the plane at the last moment. Finally, the plane took off. At that moment everyone burst out laughing, though nothing funny had happened. The laughter must have been caused by the sudden release from tension. The Swedish stewardess said this happened every time the plane took off for Stockholm.

My visit to the Soviet Union had the effect of making me reflect on my own political views. Although I always voted for the Democrats, I took no active part in American politics. I thought of myself as a cosmopolitan, but I did not subscribe to any worldwide ideology. The one belief that I did hold to firmly was pacifism. A horror of war that went back to early childhood was probably the respect in which my father had most influenced me.

I considered myself to be a liberal, though I would have had difficulty in defining what the term meant. It included, of course, such elements as a belief in the freedom of speech, the freedom of association, the freedom to travel. I was fully aware of injustices in the society in which I lived, and I realized that to the hungry man the freedom of speech might bring little comfort, but nonetheless democracy certainly was preferable to any other system.

I detested fascism in the various forms it took, before and during the war. After the war, when I went to Spain, I had been repelled by the sinister-looking police prowling the streets and by the omnipresent, haughty portraits of Franco pasted on every wall and telegraph pole. I was equally repelled by what I knew of Communism, though it seemed preferable to fascism because, in theory at least, it was dedicated to improving the lives of the common people and not to conquering other countries.

I had never had any direct experience of Communism until I visited the Soviet Union, but when I was a university student I had heard left-wing classmates denounce bourgeois democracy and its contradictions. They seemed sure the Soviet Union provided a model for America to follow, and they had ready explanations for the necessity of a dictatorship of the proletariat and even for the notorious trials that had shocked the rest of the world.

I found their arguments so unconvincing and uncongenial that when the Soviet Union invaded Finland in 1940, I was delighted to witness these left-wing classmates' embarrassment. They had always insisted that only capitalist countries ever committed acts of aggression and believed it was inconceivable that the Soviet Union would be guilty of this crime. The attack on Finland showed they were wrong. My joy, I now see, was foolish. As a pacifist, I should have been more concerned that this war might lead to others, and the initial successes of the Finnish defenders should have worried rather than pleased me because they suggested that the Russians might be unable to withstand a German attack. The signing of the nonaggression treaty between the Soviet Union and Germany shocked and baffled everyone, even the most committed believers in the Soviet Union.

My visit to this country, though brief, changed my suppositions about its people. I had expected the Russians to be fanatically convinced of the superiority of their system, sure that (as Nikita Khrushchev had declared at the United Nations) they would "bury" the bourgeois countries. To my surprise, I found that it was easy to converse with people, and I detected not the slightest sign of fanaticism. I liked almost everyone, with the exception of customs officials and hotel employees. As might be expected, I felt particularly close to the scholars of Japanese.

We were, however, separated by differences of experience. I often felt aware of how protected my life had been from the ordeals they had known. They by no means dramatized their experiences, but sometimes I could infer their bitter memories from only a few words. Once, when describing a hotel in Tokyo with unusually small rooms, I said, "They are like jail cells." The scholar with whom I was talking said merely, "No, not like jail cells." She did not elaborate, but I sensed behind her words that she may have spent months or even years in prison.

Again, when Professor Pinus related her experiences during the Germans' terrible siege of Leningrad, she mentioned that so many people had been killed that they had to be buried in mass graves. She did not know where her parents were buried. Although she spoke in unemotional tones, I shuddered to hear her words. I had never known mental anguish of this kind.

Perhaps the greatest difference separating these scholars from me was that they were not free to travel abroad. Even if they were invited to another country and provided with a ticket and the necessary papers, at the last moment they might be detained at the airport without explanation. I felt I wanted to help such people. Although I could not help them in any concrete manner, at least I could visit them from time to time so that they would feel more in touch with the outside world. I went back to the Soviet Union three more times, but I have no idea whether these visits brought any comfort.

One happy experience from a later visit stands out. My book *The Japanese Discovery of Europe* was published in Russian in an edition of 7,500 copies. It sold out the first day. There was no second printing because that would not have been in keeping with a planned economy. While in Moscow I was told that I would be paid royalties in rubles that could be used only in the Soviet Union. I didn't actually receive the money until the day before I left. With the rubles in my pocket, I went to what was perhaps the most expensive shop in Moscow and asked to see its most expensive article. I was shown a massive silver bracelet. I purchased it without hesitation, reasoning that a bracelet was better than paper money. Once I had the bracelet, however, I realized I did not know what to do with it. In the end, I gave it to Abe Machi (Abe Kōbō's wife), who, as an artist, would be intrigued by even something so impractical as a very heavy, ugly silver bracelet.

So much has changed. I visited Spain again about five years ago and was startled to see how much more cheerful and prosperous the country is than under Franco. A short visit to St. Petersburg this year produced a similar impression. No doubt there are people in both countries who resent the changes, and I am told that improvements in the major cities have not been nationwide. But who could have predicted thirty years ago that cruise ships filled with tourists would be docking every day in Russian and Spanish ports? Or that Russian tourists would be so numerous in the famous cities of Europe and America that guidebooks in Russian would be displayed at every kiosk?

I often think sadly of how much worse the world has grown. The newspapers each day report events that depress me, especially when my own country is involved. Leonard Woolf (the husband of the novelist Virginia Woolf) wrote a book entitled *Downhill All the Way* describing the changes for the worse that had occurred since the First World War. I often recall this book, but sometimes, despite a seemingly inevitable tendency, things do get better.

I shall never forget a performance of Beethoven's opera *Fidelio* at the Metropolitan in 1941. It was the worst time of the war, and the hearts of most Americans went out to the Europeans trapped, as it were, in a vast prison. Beethoven's music brought hope, and when the prison gates opened and the pale, haggard prisoners emerged, the audience, finding in the music a promise that Europe would again be free, gave themselves to tears. Amid the tremendous applause, we wept as I have never before or since seen an audience weep. And the prison gates of Europe did eventually open.

The 1960s were full of events directly related to me. The most dramatic was the student strike at Columbia in 1968, when the peace of the university was shattered by confrontations between students and faculty. The students occupied many university buildings, and the faculty, at endless meetings, debated the appropriate response. Professors who were normally reticent to utter opinions not relating to their special field were loquacious in their praise or condemnation of the strike. A great scholar who had come to America as a refugee from Germany recalled in a voice trembling with emotion how Nazi students had taken over the university where he taught. He expressed fear that the strike might be the prologue to a similar destruction of Columbia's liberal traditions. Professors sympathetic to the strike declared that Columbia's example would serve as a model for other universities; those who opposed the strike warned that parents would hesitate to send their sons to a university where teaching was likely to be interrupted in this way.

It is hard now to remember the specific issues of the strike, though opposition to the war in Vietnam was paramount. More than the details, though, I remember how pained I was when some of my students joined in the strike. Although I sympathized with them in their anger, I did not believe that preventing professors from teaching would rectify injustices. Thus I was gratified when, in the midst of the strike, at the students' request, I resumed teaching, though in my home and not in a classroom. Although the strike was initially upsetting, it in fact created surprising warmth between the students and me. Today, my closest friends among my former students date from that time.

The strike did not serve as a prelude to a student takeover of the university, nor did it lead to more "democratic" methods of teaching. Soon the professors built new ivory towers where they could continue their research undisturbed. Before long, the students, having won the right to participate in the administration of the university, lost interest in this privilege, and many resumed their customary enthusiasm for sports and rock music. The strike was symptomatic of the dissatisfaction felt by young people in many countries with the way the world was being run. Today, however, when (in my opinion) there are far more compelling reasons for dissatisfaction, the young seem oddly silent.

My memories of the 1960s have blurred, but a record of my activities exists in the form of books I published. In 1961 my translation of eleven plays by Chikamatsu Monzaemon appeared. In 1967 I published the translation of another classic, *Tsurezuregusa* (*Essays in Idleness*), my own favorite among my translations. The modern works I translated included Mishima Yukio's novel *Utage no ato* (*After the Banquet*, 1965) and his play *Sado kōshaku fujin* (*Madame de Sade*, 1967). I also published a translation of Abe Kōbō's play *Tomodachi* (*Friends*, 1969). In 1961 I published *The Old Woman, the Wife and the Archer*, a volume consisting of translations of three novellas that treat the Japanese past—Fukasawa Shichirō's *Narayama-bushi kō* (*The Songs of Oak Mountain*), Uno Chiyo's *Ohan*, and Ishikawa Jun's *Shion monogatari* (*Asters*). In addition, as I have mentioned, I published a book on bunraku and another on nō.

The saddest event of the 1960s was the death in 1964 of Tsunoda Ryūsaku, my sensei. When he learned that he was suffering from cancer, he decided to return to Japan, in order to die there. Instead, he died on the journey, in Honolulu, in the place he had first lived after leaving Japan. There was a Buddhist service in New York. As I looked at the photograph of Tsunoda-sensei above the altar, I was overcome with both gratitude and grief.

The 1960s were also the time when I came in contact with the literary world of Europe. Barney Rosset, the owner of Grove Press (which had published my anthologies of Japanese literature), invited me to be a member of the American jury of the Formentor Prize. Although I had not previously heard of this prize, it was second only to the Nobel Prize in its influence. The award of the prize in 1961 to Jorge Luis Borges and Samuel Beckett had brought both writers their first worldwide acclaim.

There were two prizes. The international prize was awarded to a recent work by a writer at the peak of his career (unlike the Nobel Prize, which generally is awarded to authors who have long since written their best works). The other prize was given to a book by a new writer. Funds for the prizes were contributed by publishers of six groups of European countries and one American company. (Chūō kōron sha joined in 1967.) The members of the seven juries were chosen without respect to nationality.

The first meeting I attended was held in 1965 in Salzburg, Austria. The American jury, partly under persuasion from me, decided to back Mishima Yukio for the international prize. However, the redoubtable American writer Mary McCarthy, a member of the British jury, made an impassioned speech in favor of *The Golden Fruits* by the French novelist Nathalie Sarraute, declaring that it was a classic from the moment it was born. The Spaniards and the Scandinavians favored the Polish novelist Witold Gombrowicz, but his chances of winning the prize were adversely affected when a member of the German jury called attention to Gombrowicz's racial prejudices.

The jurors delivered speeches on the work they supported for the prize. When the American jury's turn came, I was about to speak when I noticed that some jurors had stood and were heading for the door. I guessed this was not because of their aversion to me (I was unknown to them), but because of the attitude, fashionable at the time even among some who knew English well, of pretending not to understand it. This was one way of indicating their dislike of America.

I made up my mind on the spot to speak in French. I had never before delivered a speech in French, and I had used the language very little in recent years, but a miracle occurred. I spoke French better than ever before in my life. I don't know how this happened. No doubt (despite the miracle) my French was full of errors, but the jurors who had headed for the door returned to their seats. I don't remember now what I said in dispraise of Sarraute, whose novel I had disliked, or about Mishima and his novel *After the Banquet*, which I proposed for the prize, but after I finished talking, I could tell that I had made an impression on the members of the other juries. To my great surprise, Roger Caillois came up to me and revealed that the French jury was not solidly behind Sarraute. He told me that he thought "we" would win the prize for Mishima, I was overjoyed. I could hardly wait to send Mishima a telegram.

Alas, it did not work out that way. The Spanish jury, which had been backing Gombrowicz, shifted to Sarraute, giving her a majority and frustrating my dreams. I tried twice more, at meetings of the Formentor Prize juries held in 1966 in the south of France and in 1967 in Tunis, to persuade the different juries that Mishima, more than anyone else, deserved the prize. But these attempts failed, perhaps because (as one juror told me) I seemed overly determined to win the prize for Mishima, thereby irritating people, who thought I made a poor loser.

After my failure in Tunis, a senior member of the Swedish publishing company Bonniers, aware of my disappointment, consoled me, "Mishima will win a much more important prize very soon." This could only be the Nobel Prize. I was so pleased by his words that I forgot the sting of defeat. I could hardly wait to reach Japan and tell Mishima the good news. I knew he wanted the Nobel Prize more than anything else in the world.

Japan's turn to win the Nobel Prize in Literature arrived in 1968, but Kawabata Yasunari, and not Mishima, received it. The award to Kawabata of this most esteemed of literary awards was an occasion for rejoicing, but it may have contributed to the deaths of both men.

33

The first important event of the next decade, at least for me, was Mishima's death on November 25, 1970. As soon as details of his suicide were reported, men from the world of politics and literature were asked their opinions. The prime minister declared that it was the act of a madman. Writers, imagining what might drive themselves to suicide, guessed that Mishima had killed himself because he was unable to write. Some proudly revealed that Mishima had been a *kokoro no tomo* (bosom friend).

I was not a *kokoro no tomo* of Mishima. From the beginnings of our friendship seventeen years earlier, he had made it clear that he did not desire what he called "sticky" relations. We did not share secrets or ask each other for advice. We enjoyed meeting and conversing, whether about literature, the state of the world, or mutual acquaintances. It was a working friendship as well. I translated not only Mishima's serious works of fiction and plays but also amusing essays he wrote for American magazines.

Our relations were always rather formal. This was mainly my doing. He once asked that we drop the polite language and talk in the informal manner of old friends, but I found this difficult and somehow unnatural. I did not grow up in Japan and had never spoken Japanese to my family or classmates. Therefore, calling Mishima *kun* instead of *san* would not have made me feel any closer and might have sounded affected. Mishima, noticing that I did not respond to his request, never again asked me to speak more informally.

Although we unquestionably were friends, his politeness was unfailing and extended to every aspect of our relationship. He was my only Japanese friend who always answered my letters promptly. He was never late for an appointment. When he invited me to dinner, it was invariably to a fine restaurant, even though I often suggested we eat in less expensive places. His conversation gave me greater pleasure than any meal. While eating, we laughed a great deal. Sometimes his laugh rang out so loudly that other diners in the restaurant turned in our direction. Yoshida Ken'ichi once said that Mishima laughed with his mouth but not with his eyes. Perhaps this was true, but sincere or not, Mishima's laughter was infectious.

In the summer of 1970 Mishima invited me to Shimoda, where he customarily spent August with his family. He normally wrote every day from midnight to six, slept from six to two, then went to kendō practice or some other gathering until it was time to return home and start writing again. He spent little time with his children, but he made up for the neglect by devoting the month of August to them.

I almost canceled my trip to Shimoda because of a painful attack of *gikkuri-goshi* (slipped disk), but I was instinctively certain that Mishima had planned every moment of my stay in Shimoda from arrival to departure, and I could not bear to upset his plans. On the train I debated whether or not to mention my *gikkuri-goshi*, but when I saw him on the platform, sunburned and cheerful, I decided I would act like a samurai and keep the pain to myself.

We had lunch at a sushi restaurant. Mishima ordered only the most expensive fish. Later I was able to guess the reason: he had no time to waste on lesser fish. That evening we were joined by the journalist Henry Scott Stokes, who later wrote a book about Mishima. Mishima took us to a restaurant where lobsters were served out of season. He ordered five dinners for the three of us. But when the five dinners appeared, he ordered two more, not satisfied with the quantity. I thought this was peculiar, but no doubt he wanted to be sure we would have our fill of lobster at our last meal together.

The next day Mishima and I went to the hotel pool. He did not go in the water, but he was pleased to display his muscular body. We talked about his tetralogy *The Sea of Fertility*, which was approaching completion. He said he had put into the work everything he had learned as a writer, adding with a laugh that the only thing left was to die. I laughed too, but I must have sensed something was wrong. Violating our pledge not to discuss "sticky" matters, I asked, "If something is troubling you, why not tell me?" He averted his glance and said nothing. But he knew that three months later he would be dead.

That night in his hotel room he put into my hands the manuscript of the last chapter of the fourth volume of the tetralogy. He said he had written it in *hitoiki* (one breath). He asked if I would like to read it, but I declined, supposing I would not understand it without knowing what had happened in preceding chapters. Although it was written in August, he would inscribe the date November 25 on the manuscript, just before heading for the Self-Defense Headquarters.

I left Japan for New York in September. Departure time for the plane was ten in the morning, and I was greatly surprised when Mishima appeared to see me off. He was unshaven and his eyes were bloodshot. He probably had not slept that night. It still did not occur to me that his unusual behavior, both in Shimoda and at the airport, foreshadowed a calamity. After my plane left, Mishima went to the airport restaurant with other friends who had seen me off. He startled everyone by suddenly declaring that he refused to die a "stupid death."

That was the last time I saw Mishima. He sent a few letters to me in New York, one in response to my query as to why he had given the tetralogy the title *The Sea of Fertility*. I was then writing about him and wanted to be sure I had understood the meaning. He wrote, "The title *The Sea of Fertility* alludes to the waterless sea of that name on the moon, a sea that is no sea. One might go so far as to say it is superimposing on cosmic nihilism the image of the plenitude of the sea. There is no harm if it suggests the Zen saying 'Time is a sea.' "

I still was not sure I understood the title, but I sensed something disquieting and even ominous. Had Mishima come to the conclusion that the world was as empty of significance as the Sea of Fertility is of water?

This was his next-to-last letter. The last arrived two days after his death. It had been left on his desk when he and members of the Tate no kai set out for Ichigaya.

About midnight on the night of the incident, the telephone rang in my apartment in New York. The call was from a *Yomiuri* reporter in Washington. He informed me briefly what had taken place a few hours earlier in Tokyo and asked my impressions. I was too stunned to make a coherent reply. The telephone rang all night long, many reporters from Japanese newspapers and magazines calling. Each asked the same question, and my response gradually grew more articulate until I felt as if I were reciting lines from a play.

Although I wanted to go to Japan at once, I had no money. Then I heard that an international conference on Asian studies was to be held in January in Australia. Travel expenses were available, and it would be possible to return from Australia by way of Japan.

I obtained the grant and spent a pleasant week in Australia, but my thoughts went constantly to Japan. I arrived in Tokyo just before Mishima's funeral on January 24 and agreed to speak at the service. My three closest friends insisted, however, that I not attend lest it be thought I was speaking on behalf of Mishima's right-wing ideology. I finally yielded, but in the years since I have many times regretted I did not show more courage.

I visited Mrs. Mishima and placed on the altar under Mishima's photograph my translation of *Chūshingura*, dedicated to him. It bore an epigraph from the play he had chosen in Shimoda: *Kuni osamatte bushi no chū mo buyū mo kakururu ni, tatoeba hoshi no hiru miezu yoru wa midarete arawaruru* (When a country is at peace, the loyalty and courage of its soldiers remain hidden but, like the stars, though invisible by day, at night they reveal themselves, scattered over the firmament).

Mishima's funeral at the Tsukiji hongan-ji was presided over by Kawabata Yasunari. Even as a boy, he had participated in so many funerals that he became known as a "master of funerals," but this must have been a particularly painful occasion. Kawabata, one of the first to recognize Mishima's literary gifts, wrote in a letter sent to Mishima in 1957 that he felt sure that if he survived in the history of Japanese literature, it would be as the person who "discovered" Mishima.

I met Kawabata during my first year in Japan while he was the president of the PEN Club. His involvement in running an international organization seemed to contradict the impression he gave of unworldliness, but in fact he continued almost to the end of his life to attend international literary conferences, and he was even active politically, riding about the streets of Tokyo aboard a sound car in support of a candidate for the governorship.

I asked Kawabata's help in obtaining permissions from authors whose works I planned to use in my anthologies of Japanese literature, and he quickly got in touch with each. Quite apart from my gratitude for this and other kindnesses, I felt close to him from the first time we met. I never experienced any trouble conversing with him, though I had heard the story that his protracted silences had reduced one woman reporter to tears. He was generous with his time even when he had more pressing things to do.

I remember particularly an occasion when I visited Kawabata in Karuizawa. I had been told that as the result of the sleeping pills he took in order to overcome his chronic insomnia, he did not rise until very late. So I went at two in the afternoon, judging this was late enough. Kawabata was about to have breakfast. He invited me to join him, but I had already eaten lunch. As we talked, I noticed a man pacing back and forth in the garden. I wondered whether he was a bodyguard. Finally, unable to suppress my curiosity, I asked Kawabata who the man was, and he answered with a smile that the man had been sent by a newspaper to pick up that day's installment of the serial Kawabata was writing. Even the presence of the impatient man in the garden did not induce Kawabata to cut short our conversation.

I tended to think of Kawabata in terms of the understatement of his writings, of his devotion to Japanese traditions, and of his love for the Japanese landscape. But he had quite different aspects to his literary life as well. Early in his career he had practiced Surrealism and stream-of-consciousness techniques, and he never renounced this interest, as is clear from one of his last works of fiction, the astonishing "One Arm." Moreover, despite his love of the Japanese literature of the past, his fiction is set in the present, and he never made the modern-language translation of *The Tale of Genji* he had planned.

Something in Kawabata craved solitude, but he also enjoyed going to Tokyo bars. Once, quite by accident, we met in a bar. The next time I saw him he expressed pleasure in having seen me there, as he had been afraid I was too serious.

On another occasion, I had an unexpected glimpse into his private life. A hostess in a bar asked if it was true I had a house in

Karuizawa. Although I was surprised by the question, I admitted that I had. She surprised me even more by saying, "I have a favor to ask I can't ask of anyone else. Please do it. I'll clean your house or do anything else you ask." We agreed to meet the next day at my hotel.

She appeared as promised and gave me a letter. She asked that when I was next in Karuizawa that I give it to Kawabata, adding that it should be when Mrs. Kawabata was not present. I accepted the letter, though I felt uncomfortable. I took it with me to Karuizawa and had it in my pocket when I visited Kawabata. At a certain moment Mrs. Kawabata went into the kitchen. This was my chance, but I stopped. I had no idea of the contents of the letter, but from the manner of the hostess, it probably contained something that would upset Mrs. Kawabata. Because I felt affection for her but not for the hostess, I did not give it to him. I often have mulled over my decision. Did I act out of cowardice? Did I deprive Kawabata of comfort in his loneliness? And why did I not refuse the hostess's request in the first place?

I shall never know the answers to these questions. I had inadvertently become involved in the private life of a great man and lacked the wisdom to act with assurance.

The award of the Nobel Prize in Literature to Kawabata came as a great surprise, not because I thought he was unworthy, but because I was convinced Mishima would receive it. I had heard that after reading the translation of *The Temple of the Golden Pavilion*, Dag Hammarskjöld had expressed his admiration to the Swedish Academy, and a recommendation from this source was not to be taken lightly. I also was told by a leading Swedish publisher after Mishima failed to obtain the Formentor Prize that he would receive an even superior prize. It had not occurred to me that another Japanese might be honored.

It did not take long, however, for me to rejoice that the Nobel Prize had gone to Kawabata. He certainly deserved this recognition. But I still wondered what had induced the Swedish Academy to award the prize to Kawabata rather than Mishima. In the following year, 1969, I was invited to dinner in Copenhagen at a friend's house. One of the other guests was a man I had met in Tokyo at the time of the PEN Club Congress in 1957. On the basis of the few weeks he spent in Japan he had apparently established a reputation as an expert in Japanese literature and his views were sought by the Nobel Prize Committee. Recalling this, he announced to the gathering, "I won the prize for Kawabata!" This man, of extremely conservative political views, had decided that because Mishima was relatively young, he must be a radical. He therefore spoke strongly against Mishima and in favor of Kawabata, in the end convincing the committee.

Did this really happen? It seemed so absurd that Mishima should have been deprived of the prize because he was taken for a left-wing radical that I couldn't resist telling Mishima. He did not laugh.

Kawabata, delighted to win the prize, composed for the ceremony the moving lecture "Japan, the Beautiful, and Myself." He became a hero in Japan, and publishers vied to produce commemorative volumes of his writings. However, apart from the set of eighteenth-century Swedish chairs in his dining room, there was little visible change in Kawabata's life. Unfortunately, he no longer seemed able to write anything that would confirm his reputation as a Nobel Prize laureate. He started many works that he did not finish.

Mishima expressed his joy over Kawabata's success, and he no doubt was sincere. But he knew that the geographical factor

in the award of the Nobel Prize in Literature would prevent another Japanese from winning it for at least twenty years, and he
did not choose to wait. He threw himself into martial activities.
In November 1969 he and his little army staged a "parade" on
the roof of the National Theater. Kawabata, invited to attend, refused. I heard at the time that the angry Mishima was telling
people that he now realized Tanizaki was a greater writer than
Kawabata. He may have been overwrought with thoughts of his
impending death. Although the hope of winning the Nobel
Prize had kept him from suicide, this hope now had been dashed
and his "lifework," the final tetralogy, was approaching its end;
the path toward death was unobstructed.

Kawabata was dismayed by Mishima's death. He may have
felt that an injustice had been done, that Mishima, rather than
he, should have received the prize. Unable to write anything
that satisfied himself, he devoted himself to such projects as
promoting an international appreciation of Japanese literature,
and he was an organizer of the congress of foreign scholars of
Japanese literature held in the autumn of 1972. The last time I
saw him, he spoke with enthusiasm about the congress, but he
committed suicide six months before it began. Ōoka Shōhei said
that the Nobel Prize had killed both Mishima and Kawabata.

In 1972 a conference was sponsored by the newspaper *Asahi
shinbun* on the subject of "Greenery," and all the speakers
stressed the importance of greenery to urban life. As expected,
nobody advocated a wholesale cutting down of trees. The par-
ticipants were rewarded by being invited afterward to a restaurant where broiled eels and limitless amounts of saké were
waiting for them. At some point Shiba Ryōtarō, seated at the op-

posite end of the restaurant, got up and made his way to the table of the editor in chief of the *Asahi*. He evidently had consumed
a fair amount of saké and announced in a loud voice, "The *Asahi*
is no good."

Naturally, the editor in chief was startled. Shiba continued,
"In the Meiji period the *Asahi* was no good, but by hiring Natsume Sōseki it became a good newspaper. The only way to
make the *Asahi* a good newspaper now is to hire Donald
Keene."

I only later discovered what Shiba had in mind. Everyone
who wrote for the *Asahi* was Japanese. Shiba believed that if
there were non-Japanese employees whose desks were side by
side with the Japanese staff and who ate in the same lunchroom,
it would make it a genuinely international newspaper.

All of us, however, took this as a joke induced by the saké
Shiba had consumed. I knew I was totally incapable of performing heroic deeds in the role of the second Natsume Sōseki. But
about a week later, Nagai Michio (at the time an editorial writer
for the *Asahi*) informed me that the newspaper had decided to
follow Shiba's advice. I was offered a position as a guest editor. I
was astonished but also highly honored, and although I had
doubts about my qualifications, I accepted.

At first the *Asahi* people did not know what to do with me. I
was given a fine office of my own, but this made me invisible to
everyone else (contrary to Shiba's hopes), and there was nothing
to do there. Finally, to my relief, I was given a task, to write a series of articles on questions I was commonly asked by Japanese.
The serial, called *Nihonjin no shitsumon* (*Questions Asked by Japanese*), was well received, and this success led to my writing three
lengthy serials during the ten years I worked for the *Asahi*.

The first of these serials, *Travelers of a Hundred Ages*, was a
study of the diaries written by Japanese from the ninth to the
nineteenth century. I had been interested in Japanese diaries
ever since my wartime work as a translator, when for months at

a time I read nothing but the diaries and letters of Japanese soldiers picked up on the battlefields. It occurred to me that a study of diaries, particularly those of a personal nature, might provide valuable insights into how, over the centuries, Japanese had viewed the world around them. The serial appeared five days a week, a pace sometimes difficult to maintain. Although I wrote my manuscript in English, it was well translated by my friend Kanaseki Hisao. To my surprise and joy, the book won the prizes offered by both the *Yomiuri shinbun* and Shinchōsha for the year's best work of nonfiction.

My next serial was a sequel, continuing my account of Japanese diaries up to the 1920s. This one was more interesting for me to write because, unlike the classics of diary literature, the diaries I discussed were largely unknown. But even though in some places the diaries were close to pornographic, this serial failed to attract the attention of the earlier book. My third and last serial, *Koe no nokori* (*Lingering Voices*), about Japanese authors I have known, was much praised while it was appearing, but the book sold poorly, perhaps because of the title. My connection with the *Asahi* ended in 1992 when I retired at the age of seventy.

In the following year I published the final volume of my history of Japanese literature. Some friends spoke of it as my "life-work." Even though this was intended as praise, the words had an ominous ring, suggesting that I had reached my peak and would write nothing of equal importance in the future. I was seventy-one. In the past this would have been considered a venerable age, a time to take things easy, to putter in one's garden, or perhaps to compose haiku, but I did not feel ready for retirement. Furthermore, I did not detect in myself (though I was obviously not an impartial observer) the usual signs of old age and imminent decrepitude. In short, I wanted to continue writing.

The difficulty lay in finding a suitable subject. An editor urged me to write a book about Mishima, but fearing that this would involve a search into his private life, I decided against it. I hesitated for the same reason to write about living authors. I did not wish to know their secrets, and I thought it likely that even if I lauded 90 percent of a man's writings, he would resent any criticism of the remaining 10 percent.

At this point a magazine editor asked me for an article concerning my next book. I still had not settled on a subject, but when I started to write, I thought of a possibility. I could write a biography of a Japanese, not a contemporary and not a literary man. But which one? It came to me that although Emperor Meiji was acclaimed as the greatest of the Japanese monarchs, there was no biography of him in English, and even in Japanese there were very few. He obviously merited one.

I was fully aware that apart from having read literary works of the Meiji era, I had no qualifications as a biographer. Fortunately, some months earlier I had bought a set of the thirteen volumes of *Meiji tennō ki* (*Record of Emperor Meiji*), attracted less by the subject than by the unusually inexpensive price. This set would serve as my chief guide during the next five years while I wrote the biography.

I decided I would begin the biography with Emperor Meiji's father, Emperor Kōmei. I knew little about him, but I remembered that my teacher, Tsunoda Ryūsaku, had told me that around 1915 at a bar in Honolulu, he had met a Japanese who said he had been exiled because of his part in Kōmei's assassination. This story had stuck in my memory, though I could not use it in the biography: my memory of Tsunoda's story, heard forty years earlier, may have been faulty; his memory of the man in the bar in Honolulu another forty years earlier may also have been untrustworthy; and the man himself may have been drunk. But the existence of such a rumor aroused my curiosity, and the more I read about Kōmei, the more absorbing a figure he became. As a result of this interest, I devoted the first fifth of my biography of Emperor Meiji to events in his father's reign.

Of course, an important feature of that reign was the birth of Emperor Meiji, and I described his life from the day he was born: the rituals accompanying his birth, the consultations with masters of yin-yang, the clothes in which the infant was dressed, the traditional toys he received. Although such details are of scant interest to professional historians, they communicated to me, more vividly than accounts of political or economic changes, the differences separating life in Japan in the year of Meiji's birth from life there today.

My biography was unlike the usual studies of the period in that I included many poems composed by people around the future emperor when he was still a boy and, later, by the emperor himself. Most of his poems are on familiar, even hackneyed, themes, but occasionally they enable us to hear his voice. Such clues are precious because unlike Kōmei, Meiji left no memorable letters, and the people who knew him best rarely described aspects of his private life. It was difficult to make a biography come alive with only a few personal details, but in the course of my search, I think I came fairly close to Emperor Meiji.

The success of my biography of Emperor Meiji was, of course, gratifying. I had not expected it, even though my translator, Kakuchi Yukio, predicted from the first that it would sell 100,000 copies. (It actually sold more than 60,000.) I was especially pleased when a Korean and a Russian translation were published. But in one respect the success brought me embarrassment.

The book was written at the suggestion of the publisher Shinchōsha, and at every stage of writing this long book I had the valuable help of its editors. I cannot imagine any publisher could have done more for an author. However, one day conversing with Shimanaka Masako, I felt a pang of guilt that I had not chosen to publish the book with Chūō kōron sha. Her late husband, Shimanaka Hōji, the former president of this company, not only had been a close friend but also had given me a start in the Japanese literary world, and even when there was opposition within his company to the preferential treatment I received, he did not swerve in his kindness. He published my history of Japanese literature in eighteen volumes, probably at a loss. And yet I had allowed my first really successful book to be published elsewhere.

I promised Mrs. Shimanaka that she (who had become the president of Chūō kōron sha after her husband's death) would have my next book. I asked her what I should write about. She answered, "*Nihon no kokoro.*"

Of course I was familiar with this phrase. I had heard it many times, though I had never considered precisely what people meant when they spoke of "the heart of Japan." I thought of what it meant for me. The first thing that came to my mind was a typical Japanese room with tatami covering the floor, shōji (paper doors), a tokonoma (alcove) containing an ink painting and a flower arrangement, and, just outside, an unobtrusive garden that is an essential part of the room. This kind of room in a restaurant satisfies an aesthetic yearning of the Japanese and induces them to pay high prices for what is a relatively simple meal. The intimacy created by the simple elegance is perhaps the greatest attraction of such a room, even more than the flower arrangement, though the flowers contribute to the atmosphere. Even a man who finds it a strain to sit on the floor rather than on a chair will gladly attend a meal served here, and he probably will not worry that long squatting may cause wrinkles in his trousers. A room of this description certainly belongs to *Nihon no kokoro.*

I thought of other possible elements. The understated simplicity of the nō drama came to mind. The austere setting, the stylized movements, the ritualized delivery that never drops into vulgar realism, and the timeless themes are distinctively Japanese and quite unlike either Chinese or modern Western drama, though they bear some resemblance to ancient Greek theater. But having decided that nō should be included in *Nihon no kokoro*, it occurred to me that kabuki is no less Japanese, even though it is totally unlike nō with its colorful sets and exaggerated delivery and gestures. Moreover, unlike the timeless world of nō, kabuki is closely associated with a particular period of Japanese history.

Similar contradictions are likely to surface whenever one makes generalizations about any aspect of Japanese taste. If one decides that Japanese architecture is marked by simplicity and an absence of decoration, how then to explain the exuberantly decorated Tōshōgū at Nikkō, considered by many Japanese as a splendid example of architecture? If one decides that ink painting most closely accords with *Nihon no kokoro*, how does one reconcile this with *The Tale of Genji* scrolls, considered the supreme masterpieces of Japanese painting, despite their brilliant colors? If the rough texture and subdued coloring of Bizen pottery seem most typical of the Japanese, should one then exclude more colorful ceramics from *Nihon no kokoro*?

Of course, Japanese taste has not remained unchanged over the centuries, and probably there is no definition of *Nihon no kokoro* that can be applied to every period of Japanese history and to every layer of society. But if one agrees that a typical room in an expensive Japanese restaurant is an example of *Nihon no kokoro*, it is possible to name its distinctive features and to trace their origins, though we must not forget that quite contradictory manifestations of Japanese taste can also be included under the rubric of *Nihon no kokoro*.

Scholars frequently mention the fifteenth-century Ōnin War as the dividing period between the old and new in Japanese culture. During this war, which lasted for ten years from 1467 to 1477, virtually every building in the city of Kyoto was destroyed. At that time, Kyoto was not merely the biggest city in Japan but the great repository of Japanese culture, and its destruction was an immense, irreplaceable loss. When the war finally ended, it must have seemed impossible that the city could ever be rebuilt and regain its old grandeur, but five years later construction began on Ashikaga Yoshimasa's retreat at Higashiyama, the starting point of a new culture that survives today not only in the furnishing of fancy restaurants but in every building with even one Japanese-style room.

The *shoin-zukuri*, the most typical style of Japanese architecture, was created at Higashiyama. One distinctive feature of this style is the use of square rather than round pillars. Tatami mats, another feature, existed as far back as the Heian period, as we know from paintings, but generally only a few tatami were scattered in a room; not until the Higashiyama era did they cover the entire floor. The shōji and the tokonoma, two features of every Japanese room, originated in the same era.

The style of paintings also changed: earlier paintings usually were in color, but from this time onward, ink paintings became more typical of Japanese taste. Again, Japanese had long offered flowers to the gods and buddhas, but the art of flower arrangement was unknown until Yoshimasa's time. And it may have been in a room that still exists in the Ginkaku-ji, the temple built by Yoshimasa, that the tea ceremony was born.

I had not realized the central role of the Higashiyama culture until I began my study of *Nihon no kokoro*. Accounts of Yoshimasa I had read in histories of Japan had led me to believe that he was a capricious tyrant who amused himself by admiring his art treasures while Kyoto was burning in the Ōnin War. I thought he probably was like Nero, who (supposedly) played a violin as the city of Rome was sacked by the barbarians. I was wrong. Especially in his later years, Yoshimasa was a sensitive and aesthetically gifted man, though until he took up residence at the Ginkaku-ji, he had contributed almost nothing to the welfare of the Japanese of his own time or to the culture of future generations. He was a failure as a shogun. His married life with Hino Tomiko was unhappy, and his relations with his son, Yoshihisa, were marred by hostility. But in the last decade of his life, he was the guiding spirit of the Higashiyama era, and the cultural legacy of that time to the Japanese people proved immense. Possibly no man in the history of Japan had a greater influence on the formation of *Nihon no kokoro*.

The text of my book was serialized in *Chūō kōron* for about a year. The only reaction I had during this time was a telephone call from Shimanaka Masako. She said laughingly that she was afraid that the contents of my serial might be too difficult for ordinary readers. This was a disappointment, and when the book appeared, there were few reviews, another disappointment. But an author is likely to feel special affection for a neglected off-spring, and when (as happens once in a while) someone praises this book, it gives far greater pleasure than the praise for my biography of Emperor Meiji.

Perhaps the most notable thing about the term *Nihon no kokoro* is that Japanese have continued to use it to convey their belief in the uniqueness of their aesthetic and spiritual heritage. They may be right in their claim of uniqueness, but Japanese culture, especially that of the Higashiyama era, is now part of the world.

During the 1980s my life tended to consist of a series of *nenchū gyōji* (annual events). New Year's Eve each year would be spent with Abe Kōbō and his wife, Machi. I wish now I had recorded our conversations or at least taken extensive notes. Everything Abe said was of interest, his serious remarks lightened by wit and especially by paradox. Mrs. Abe, no less intelligent and amusing, took a lively part in the conversation. I remember of the room only the large collection of foreign translations of Abe's works, arrayed against a wall.

The food was unconventional but essentially Japanese. Despite his cosmopolitanism, Abe liked Japanese food best of all. We usually drank saké but sometimes wine, and one year Abe proudly produced a drink of his own concoction. He asked me if I recognized it. The taste was familiar but somehow elusive. It turned out to be saké and *tansan* (sodium carbonate) mixed to produce an instant champagne. I do not recommend it.

New Year's Day was (and is) spent in Tokyo with Nagai Michio's family, eating the traditional *osechi ryōri*. I confess that this is not my favorite cuisine, but I have come to enjoy observing *nenchū gyōji*, including the food, a sure sign I have become very Japanese. The next day or the day after that, I always invite the family to Usami for a dinner at Kitchō.

Then, after a week of hasty visits to department stores to find gifts for friends in America and last glimpses of kabuki, about January 10 I board a plane for New York. I always regret my departure, and the last time I turn round at the gate to wave to the friends who have seen me off, I still wonder whether I shall be fortunate enough to return again.

Travel to and from Japan has never became routine for me; it still retains the excitement of my first glimpse from the air of the Japanese coast. It is painful to leave each January, but I must be back in New York in time for the spring semester at Columbia. Every year I have the same anxiety concerning my arrival in New York. I fear that a snowstorm may make it impossible to get from the airport to the city. Only once have I had this experience, but I am a born worrier.

Back in my apartment in New York, I look around the room. It is undoubtedly the place where I have lived for twenty years, but there is little feeling of homecoming. Yes, the shelves contain my books, some bought while I was still a high school student. In cabinets and on the floor are hundreds of LP records acquired over the years and listened to innumerable times, especially when I was lonely or depressed. The Chinese carpet on the living-room floor was purchased by my father in 1927 or 1928, just before the beginning of the Great Depression, when the family moved to a new house. Everything is familiar, but I have changed. The center of my world has moved to Japan.

New York has its attractions. My apartment looks over the Hudson River. In January, ice floes often drift by, bleak but beautiful. The coming of spring transforms the park directly below my windows. A short walk from my apartment is the East Asian Library at Columbia, where I can find almost any book

I need. In fact, I purchased many of the books in the collection in Japan. Although I enjoy buying books, those I buy tend to end up at the Columbia library rather than in my house, where there no longer is room for them. The Columbia collection also includes books given to me by authors, as well as their letters.

The chief attraction of New York is seeing old friends. Many of my closest Japanese friends have died. I used to give a party at the end of each year in my Tokyo apartment for my friends— Nagai Michio and his wife, Shimanaka Hōji and his wife, Abe Kōbō and Machi, Shinoda Hajime and his wife, Shōji Kaoru and Nakamura Hiroko, Ariyoshi Sawako, Tokuoka Takao. More than half these friends have died, though all were younger than I. But strangely, my New York friends, even some considerably older than me, are still alive, and it gives me pleasure to reminisce with them about the people we have known and the events we have shared over the fifty or sixty years since I first knew them.

New York also means the Metropolitan Opera. I first attended a performance there in 1938 when I was sixteen. The opera was Gluck's *Orfeo ed Euridice*, the oldest work in its repertory. Although I knew only a few fragments of the music and could not understand the Italian words, I was captivated, especially by the scene in which Orpheus goes down into hell to search for his wife, who has died. The music that accompanies the writhing of the denizens of hell and the contrasting music of the blessed spirits fascinated me. I had attended plays in New York ever since I was eleven or twelve, and of course I had seen many films, but nothing had moved me so much as this eighteenth-century opera.

I wanted to buy a recording of *Orfeo*, but at the time recordings of complete operas were generally on fifteen or more disks, and I could not afford them. Instead, I saved what money came my way to buy tickets for other operas. In the following year, when my mother asked what I would like for a birthday present,

I answered, "A subscription to the opera." The subscription consisted of tickets to sixteen operas on successive Fridays. The cost was minimal—a dollar for each performance—but I knew it was a strain on my mother's finances to pay the sixteen dollars, and I was deeply grateful.

It was a glorious period of opera, especially those of Wagner. My seat was in the last row of the top balcony, but I heard perfectly the thrilling voices of the Norwegian soprano Kirsten Flagstad and the Danish tenor Lauritz Melchior. Although I have attended opera many times since then and in many opera houses, I have never again heard such singing. The acting, however, was elemental. This did not bother me, however, perhaps because I was sitting so far from the stage. When as the heroic Siegfried, Melchior made a mighty leap from a height of about a foot, it would have seemed comic if not for the music. I certainly was never tempted to laugh, as I was too much in its power. In those days the sets at the Metropolitan were old and shabby, but when Flagstad came into the Hall of Song in *Tannhäuser*, her voice transformed the dusty hangings into a place of magnificence.

When I first lived in Japan, most of my friends were totally uninterested in opera, even if they knew a great deal about other kinds of music. They explained it was because they could not understand the words. Ideally, of course, one should understand every word, regardless of the language, in order to appreciate the skill with which the singer interprets the meaning. But the words of most operas are pedestrian. I can't imagine anyone reading, as one reads a work of literature, the text of an Italian opera. And from reading the text of the love duet in *Tristan und Isolde*, one surely could have no idea of the overpowering beauty of the scene when the words are sung. Rather, the special pleasure of opera, apart from the melodies, is what it reveals to us of the deepest emotions of the characters, regardless of the words. If the music of an opera succeeds in transmitting these emotions, the pleasure will be renewed every time one hears it.

At first it was not easy for me to enjoy Wagner's music, but I bought the records of Flagstad singing the final scene of *Götterdämmerung* and listened to them day after day until every note was familiar. I could hardly wait to get home from the university to listen to the music again.

These are among my happy memories of New York. It makes me sad, no doubt because of such memories, when Japanese refer to New York as a "crime city." Apart possibly from San Francisco, there is no other American city where I would wish to live.

All the same, each May, when the time for leaving New York for Tokyo approaches, I am filled with excitement at the prospect of experiencing once again this most important of my *nenjū gyōji.*

In 1981 I received the degree of Doctor of Letters from Cambridge University. This degree is granted not when the recipient has completed a dissertation or published a book but after an appraisal of his entire work to date. It was a great honor to receive this degree and to resume, after almost thirty years, my connections with Cambridge. Some professors I had known were still teaching and remembered me, but I was most affected by the greeting of the head porter of the college where I had lived. He said, "Welcome home, sir."

The ceremony of awarding the degree was carried out in keeping with Cambridge traditions dating back many years, perhaps centuries. Dressed in the appropriate gown for a Master of Arts, I knelt on a red velvet cushion before the vice-chancellor of the university. He took my hands, clasped as if in prayer, in his own and said something in Latin. I mumbled the brief, traditional reply. I felt as if I had been personally inducted into an ancient order of scholars, linking myself to many great men of the past.

Before the ceremony I had traveled with my colleague Carol Gluck and her husband, Peter, an architect, to see some of the cathedrals of England. We visited Durham, York, and Lincoln. These magnificent buildings and the countryside around them awakened an attachment to England that had been submerged under my love for Japan. I had been so eager to return to Japan each year that when I left New York I had not considered going in the opposite direction, to Europe.

During the following years I was invited on several occasions to attend conferences held in Europe, most often in Italy. In some ways Italy is maddening for tourists because almost every building they want to visit is likely to be closed, perhaps for years while under repair, but nowhere else in Europe is so filled with marvels. Venice, where I attended conferences on Tanizaki and on Hokusai, attracted me especially. I was happy to be there because, apart from the magnificent architecture and its other artistic glories, Venice is a city without cars, where the only noise heard from the streets is the sound of footsteps.

I spent a month in Paris in 1990, lecturing on Japanese diaries at the Collège de France. Although my French was no longer as fluent as in the past, it gave me pleasure to deliver the lectures, and I was extremely happy to be in Paris. I liked best of all wandering the streets without aim, remembering buildings, some not seen since 1948, as if they were old friends. I nostalgically went to have a look at the cheap hotels where I used to stay and was pleased to find they were still standing. I hoped I would also find the restaurant I had frequented in those days, where one could get a good meal for one hundred francs at a time when the dollar was worth more than three hundred francs, but it had disappeared. I went again to the glorious old opera house and recalled a performance when my view of the stage was impeded by carved wooden pineapples, part of the decoration. I remembered, with particular affection, the willow at the tip of the Ile de la Cité, the first tree to sprout leaves each spring.

My greatest adventure while living in Europe was the journey I took with three friends in a British jeep all the way from England to Istanbul, where the first postwar Congress of Orientalists was held in 1951. We and the jeep crossed the Channel by plane, then traveled through France into Italy, Yugoslavia, and Greece before reaching Turkey. We carried sleeping bags, planning to sleep in the open, in that way avoiding hotel bills, but in one small town in Yugoslavia with no likely place to spend the night outdoors, we decided to stay at a hotel. The innkeeper showed us the rooms. In the first was a big bed in which four or five men were sleeping. He told us, "There's room for one more." We slept on the floor.

Most of the bridges on our journey had been destroyed during the war. Our jeep managed to get through rivers, but afterward it took an hour for the brakes to function again. There was no road between Greece and Turkey. A man offered to guide us, and the jeep, with the man on the hood giving instructions, bounced through the fields until we could see a house in the distance. The man said, "That's Turkey." He jumped down and, refusing any money, cheerfully sauntered off. In the first Turkish village an old man asked us in English, "Are you a traveler?"

I spent about a month in Istanbul. My first reaction to the city was disappointment in the unpainted wooden houses with their peeling walls and the dreariness of the bazaar. I had expected the bazaar would be filled with rare oriental treasures, but nothing on sale remotely resembled a treasure, and loudspeakers blared out the fake orientalism of the bacchanale from the opera *Samson and Delila*. However, it took only a few days for disappointment to give way to an affection for the city so strong I thought I would happily live there for the rest of my life. I became especially fond of the old wooden houses and thought that the Aya Sofia mosque was the most beautiful building I had ever seen. I was dazzled as well by the treasures of the sultans in the Topkapi Museum.

On a fairly recent visit to Istanbul, I discovered to my amazement that all the wooden houses had disappeared. It had become a modern city. One thing that remained unaltered from fifty years earlier was the thrill of standing in Europe and looking across the Bosporus to Asia. In 1951, when I had no money for air travel, I thought this was as close to Asia as I was likely to get.

During the past fifteen years I also have visited countries I had not known before, often on the Japanese cruise ship *Asuka*. In 1998 I was invited to spend two weeks aboard the ship, one segment of its round-the-world cruise. My only obligation was to give two or three lectures in Japanese while aboard ship. Of course I was delighted. I had not traveled anywhere by ship in forty years. Often when on an airplane I had remembered how much greater pleasure it was to travel by sea.

My first cruise aboard the *Asuka* was from New York through the West Indies to the Panama Canal and from there to Acapulco in Mexico. The departure from New York on a misty evening was particularly memorable. Although I was born and raised in New York, I had never seen from the water the innumerable lights of the city as darkness fell.

I have since spent about two weeks each year on the *Asuka*. During the last few voyages I lectured not only on Japanese literature but also on opera, thus combining my interests. I have seen both the northernmost point of Norway, where the sun never sets in summer, and Manaus, a port on the Amazon just south of the equator whose greatest attraction is a splendid opera house.

I know that I have been lucky and usually feel so embarrassed by this luck that I avoid mentioning my travels to friends who have not been so fortunate. If I do have the occasion to mention my seaborne travels, I generally emphasize the fact that living aboard a ship permits me to study without the interruption of telephone calls. This is not a lie. I was able to read in my cabin three or four volumes of *Meiji tennō ki* and (on a later voyage) several books on Ashikaga Yoshimasa. But of course, that is not what has made my two weeks both on the sea and at foreign ports so enjoyable. This year the highlights were unforgettable visits to the medieval city of Tallinn in Estonia and the spectacularly beautiful St. Petersburg. During the war, it never occurred to me that a day would come when I would travel aboard a Japanese cruise ship, thanks to my ability to speak Japanese.

Does my renewed interest in other parts of the world signify a diminution in my love of Japan? The answer is definitely no. I enjoy being a tourist and often wish to spend longer in a port than the allotted day or two, but my life is so closely intertwined with Japan that I cannot conceive of cutting these ties. Japan will always be my final destination.

The counterpart of my lifelong efforts to learn as much as possible about Japan and the Japanese has been my curiosity about how Japanese have regarded foreigners over the centuries. The first foreigners of whom the Japanese were aware were the Chinese and Koreans, and contacts with these two peoples went back to the beginnings of Japanese history. Because both the Chinese and the Koreans resemble the Japanese in physical features, they tended to be distinguished from Japanese by their language and their clothes rather than by their faces. When Japanese painted pictures of scenes in China, they did not have to worry about the accuracy of their portrayals of Chinese people. The flowing robes, the unusual way of doing the hair, and (in pictures of men) the long, wispy beards were enough to convey the fact that the people in the picture were not Japanese.

The Japanese had little experience, however, of faces that were dissimilar to their own. Although they believed in Buddhism and were vaguely aware this religion had originated in India, by the time Buddhism reached Japan, the paintings and sculptures of the buddhas had East Asian faces. Only Daruma, with his big eyes and hairy chest, retained his identity as a foreigner.

After the Portuguese arrived in Japan in the middle of the sixteenth century, Japanese painters for the first time depicted foreign faces. Although the Portuguese were known as "southern barbarians" (*nanban*), artists portrayed them not as wild barbarians but as civilized human beings, even though the Portuguese had bigger noses than the Japanese and wore strange clothes. The Japanese eagerly absorbed whatever they could of the foreign culture. Fashionable young men wore Portuguese doublets, and Okuni, the legendary founder of kabuki, sported a crucifix, though not out of religious conviction. Wine became popular, and various kinds of food were introduced from both Europe and the New World. Tobacco, *kasutera* cake, sweet potatoes, and tempura cooking came at this time from abroad. Hideyoshi liked to relax in Western clothes, and his favorite food was beef stew.

For almost a century the Japanese treated the Europeans well. But the fear that Christianity might induce people to divide their loyalties between their religion and their country led to the prohibition of that religion, followed by the long period when the country was closed (*sakoku*). Thus for more than two hundred years, all that most Japanese knew about foreigners, never having seen one, was that they had red hair and green eyes. It is true that the Japanese who lived in Nagasaki might have caught a glimpse of the Dutchmen on the island of Deshima, the one place in Japan where Europeans were permitted to reside, but contacts between the Japanese and the Dutch were generally confined to the interpreters. In the eighteenth century, a few Japanese—probably not more than one hundred men—began to study Dutch in order to acquire a knowledge of European medicine, astronomy, navigation, and other branches of science.

It was extremely difficult to learn Dutch. Apart from the official interpreters on Deshima, who guarded their knowledge of Dutch as a family secret and discouraged others from attempting to learn the language, no one could help aspiring *rangakusha* (scholars of Dutch learning). There were no dictionaries, no grammars, no clues to pronunciation. Most Japanese never had the opportunity to talk with a Dutchman. Yet despite the difficulties, they persisted in their efforts to learn about the West, in the belief that this knowledge would benefit Japan.

I first learned about the *rangakusha* in Tsunoda-sensei's class on Tokugawa thought. Although his lectures enabled the students to understand the special features of each of the different schools of Confucianism, I sensed that the independent thinkers—men who did not belong to any school—appealed to him even more. I was attracted particularly to Honda Toshiaki.

Honda, an economist, pondered the causes of such calamities as the famine that followed the eruption of Mount Asana in 1783. He went to Shinano Province and was horrified by the sight of people dying of starvation. He estimated that 2 million people had died in the famine and was dismayed to see that great tracts of formerly cultivated land had turned into barren wasteland. He asked, "If these facts were known to the Europeans, would they not despise us? They would say that it is because people who live in wooden houses are stupid and of feeble intelligence that so many citizens were lost."

Honda did not merely comment on the suffering he had seen but also proposed solutions, including government control of shipping and the acquisition of foreign territories. He became convinced that Japan must follow the examples provided by the prosperous countries of the West. Sometimes, though, he went astray because of his enthusiasm for European ways, as in his statement that people who live in wooden houses are stupid, an opinion he attributed to the Dutch, or when he urged that the capital of Japan be moved to Kamchatka because it was at the same degree of latitude as London and therefore should enjoy similar prosperity.

In most respects, however, Honda was above all practical. He favored abandoning *kanji* (Japanese characters) because their large number made them inefficient. It would be preferable to use *kana* (shortened forms of characters) only, but the alphabet (with only twenty-six letters) would be even better. He admired European paintings that exactly resembled the objects portrayed, believing them to be superior to Japanese paintings, which were merely beautiful and served no useful purpose. He disliked all religions, though he wondered whether the prosperity of the Chinese port cities was not due to the adoption of Christianity.

Other Japanese were far less friendly toward the Europeans. Hirata Atsutane, who respected European science, nevertheless described the Dutch in these terms: "Their eyes are really just like a dog's. They are long from the waist downward, and the slenderness of their legs makes them resemble animals. When

they urinate, they lift one leg, the way dogs do. Moreover, apparently because the backs of their feet do not reach to the ground, they fasten wooden heels to their shoes, which makes them look all the more like dogs."

Hirata's views aroused the opposition of the *rangakusha* and are likely to strike readers today as comic, but they provide evidence that despite the efforts of the *rangakusha*, some Japanese thought of foreigners as devils or even as animals. Commodore Matthew Perry and his officers are depicted in Japanese paintings of the period of the black ships not simply as curiosities but as monsters with mouths opened wide, as if screaming maledictions. Even after the Meiji Restoration and the period of adulation of foreigners symbolized by the Rokumeikan, many Japanese continued to think of foreigners, if not in Hirata's extreme terms, then as creatures totally unlike themselves. After the Meiji Restoration, periods of admiration for foreign things regularly alternated with periods of *Nippon shugi* (Japanism).

When I arrived in Kyoto in 1953, I was thirty-one. People I met casually would often ask my age. At first I replied truthfully, but since this was not very interesting, for fun I answered on one occasion, "Sixteen." This caused one questioner to explain to his neighbor at the bar, "Foreigners have heavy beards. That makes them look older." On another occasion I said, "Fifty-five," at which the man who had asked my age shook my hand, saying, "The same as myself."

I mention these trivial incidents because a marked change has occurred. A few days ago I had an experience that would not have happened ten years ago. A woman asked me directions to the nearest subway station. I felt a moment of joy. The woman had decided that despite my face, I would know where the station was. Or perhaps I looked like an intelligent human being and she did not consider whether or not I was Japanese. The long struggle of the *rangakusha* had at last borne fruit.

40

In 2003 I began work on a subject that would have pleased Tsunoda-sensei: the painter and independent thinker Watanabe Kazan. I felt some hesitation about writing a book that would require an extensive knowledge of art, but brushing aside such doubts, I set about acquiring the materials I would need in order to write about Kazan and the late Tokugawa period. I hoped that this study would provide a background to the biography of Emperor Meiji I had published and that it might clarify the reasons why the Restoration was so successful.

The proposed book also represented a sequel to my book *The Japanese Discovery of Europe*. Thirty-seven years ago, when the Japanese translation of this book was published, a reviewer expressed the hope I would continue my study of *rangaku* (Dutch studies) into the 1830s. I had quite forgotten the review but now was unconsciously complying with the suggestion.

I decided that Kazan would be the central figure of my study, but as yet I knew little about him. I recalled two drawings by Kazan showing how harshly he was treated after being arrested for allegedly showing excessive partiality for the West. One sketch shows him squatting on the ground as he is trussed with ropes. The other sketch shows Kazan, his hands chained together, being interrogated by two sworded samurai. These sketches lingered in my memory even more than the accounts I had read of Kazan's life.

I was attracted to Kazan especially as a thinker. But I knew that he was better known as a painter and therefore began my research by examining his paintings reproduced in art books and catalogues of exhibitions. Some paintings so closely resembled earlier Chinese or Japanese paintings that they did not interest me, but even when Kazan painted conventional subjects, he was a superior artist. His portraits impressed me most.

The long tradition of portraiture in Japan dates back to the portrait of Prince Shōtoku. Portraits were often painted of emperors, Buddhist priests and nuns, shoguns and lesser warriors, and, less frequently, the wives of warriors. Often a portrait was painted after a man's death by an artist who had never seen him, but the lack of resemblance was not criticized. Instead, it was sufficient for the artist to suggest the virtue considered most characteristic of the subject, whether commanding dignity, profound piety, or unruffled calm. Although these state portraits were often well painted, the beholder is unlikely to feel the bond between himself and the person depicted that he feels when gazing at a Dutch portrait.

The portraits of Ikkyū and Hideyoshi are among the best examples of the Japanese tradition in portraiture. They are memorable, even though they lack the shading or coloring that would have imparted more realistic contours to the face. Such portraits are rather like cartoons that, although they capture the striking features of the subject's face, do not create the impression of a living person. Many portraits, like those in scrolls depicting the thirty-six immortals of poetry, are so alike that the poets' faces are distinguishable from one another mainly by the shape and size of their mustache and beard. Women poets were sometimes portrayed from behind, a cascading flow of hair taking the place of a face.

Kazan felt dissatisfied with such portraits, just as he was dissatisfied with the landscape paintings of anonymous mountains. He wrote that when painting a mountain, the artist must make it unmistakably like a particular mountain; it should not be a generic mountain. This criticism was aimed especially at Japanese artists who painted scenes of "poetic" mountains in China they had never seen, mountains that existed only in their imagination.

Kazan created a new kind of portrait that was probably influenced by illustrations in Dutch books. As far as I know, no oil portraits had been imported into Japan, but other portraits, mainly etchings, were available. Most books, even treatises on scientific subjects, were likely to have for their frontispiece a portrait of the gentleman to whom the book was dedicated. Such etchings may have suggested to Kazan how to make his portraits more like the subjects than earlier Japanese examples had been. He came to believe that realism was a painting's most essential quality, whether it was a landscape or a portrait.

The desire to make one's painting a faithful representation of the subjects was customary in the West. European painters attempted to depict accurately not only the subjects' features but also the texture of their clothes, whether silk or wool, and the fur or feathers that were part of their costumes. As we know, the Japanese were fully capable of painting with minute exactness, for example, from the drawings of insects, but their portraits lacked precision.

Kazan's resolve to achieve accuracy in his portraits is evident from the eleven preliminary studies he made for his portrait of the Confucian scholar Satō Issai. All the studies are painted from the same angle and the expression varies little from one to the next, but in each successive study Kazan attempted to come closer to capturing the individuality of Issai's face. He paid little attention to his clothes, as he was interested only in the man, and there is a vitality in Issai's face without precedent in Japan. Indeed, as depicted in Kazan's painting, Issei is not simply a learned Confucian philosopher but a particular individual as well.

Perhaps Kazan placed such importance on Issai's individuality as a reaction to the confining restrictions imposed by the feudal regime on the aspirations of the individual. He praised the Dutch system of education, which fostered students' inborn talents, unlike that of Japan in which students had to conform to the dicta of a Confucian education. As a samurai, Kazan was better off than commoners, but he was condemned to spend his days poring over domain records when all he wanted to do was to paint. He had studied Confucianism from boyhood and quoted Confucian texts repeatedly in his works, but unlike run-of-the-mill Confucian scholars, he was eager to learn from the

West, both in order to improve his paintings and to have a better understanding of the world. He wrote,

> In recent years, ever since Dutch learning became prominent, there has been a tendency for Confucian scholars to reject it, declaring that barbarian theories should not be adopted. What is the meaning of this criticism? Dutch learning is not perfect, but if we choose the good points and follow them, what harm can come of that? What is more ridiculous than to refuse to discuss its merits and to cling to what one knows best with no thought of ever changing?

Kazan compared such Confucian scholars to frogs in a well, satisfied with their narrow domain and ignorant of the world outside. He compared them also to blind men who do not fear snakes or deaf men who do not run from bolts of lightning. He feared that unless the Japanese studied the West and discovered what Japan must learn from Europe, the country would be in danger of a European invasion. He found much to admire in the Dutch books that he read in translation, not because he was intrigued by exotic information, but because he believed that the more the Japanese knew about the West, the more it would benefit Japan.

When some of Kazan's manuscripts fell into the hands of shogunate officials, he was arrested. His only crime was having praised the West, in this way implicitly criticizing Japan. He was narrowly saved from execution by the intercession of a Confucian scholar.

Kazan was sent into house arrest in Tahara (in modern Aichi Prefecture). As a vassal of the daimyo of Tahara, this was his official place of residence, even though he had spent his entire life in Edo. His exile was spent in poverty, relieved by gifts from disciples. He finally agreed to paint again and to allow the paintings to be sold. When samurai of his domain discovered this, they accused him of violating the terms of his confinement. Fearing that his actions might bring shame on the daimyo, he committed suicide.

Kazan paid the penalty for having been an independent thinker at a time when independent views were unwelcome.

When I was a boy, my father would sometimes return home drunk and rather maudlin. At such times he might lean over my bed and impart to me his conviction that human beings should die before they were fifty-five. "After that," he would add, "they are no good for anything."

I don't know why my father, who was still in his thirties, was so pessimistic about old age, but to a boy of ten or twelve, fifty-five seemed like the distant future, and I readily accepted my father's opinion as the truth. (He actually lived until his eighties, and his last were probably his happiest years.) Two experiences in my later years, however, changed my mind. The first was studying with Tsunoda-sensei, then in his seventies, and observing his love of scholarship and his joy at passing on his discoveries to his students. The second was seeing a film of Arturo Toscanini, in his late seventies, conducting a work by Verdi and transmitting his passion for the music to the orchestra. In both cases I sensed something not found in younger men, a kind of enlightenment, that deeply appealed to me. I decided not to die at fifty-five.

I now am eighty-four. In the past this would have been considered a remarkable old age, but nowadays it has become, in Japan especially, a normal lifetime. I have been very fortunate in that I have seldom been ill and, except for two brief periods, have not spent time in hospitals. I seldom worry about my health, have never willingly exercised, never tried to eat a balanced diet. Japanese friends look at me in amazement when I admit that I have no idea of my blood pressure. Even when a doctor tells me what my blood pressure is, I don't know whether I should be glad or sad.

I wonder why I have lived longer than people who take every precaution for their health and obey all the rules for a long life. Perhaps it is heredity. One of my grandmothers lived to the age of one hundred. Regardless of the cause, I am grateful and I look forward to years of activity to come. I have started to work on a new book that, if I manage to complete it, will take me at least five years. Writing this book will give me pleasure. I have not the slightest desire to sit under a palm tree gazing out at the sea, a glass of rum in my hand.

Sometimes, it is true, I fear that senility may overtake me, as it has overtaken some of my friends. There is nothing more heart-breaking than to look into the eyes of a close friend and see no sign of recognition. At the thought that I, too, might one day be able to give no more than a blank, uncomprehending stare, I feel that living in that state would be worse than death. But then I think of those who have been productive even in very old age. Verdi composed *Falstaff* at eighty. Hokusai went on painting until he was ninety. Nogami Yaeko, with whom I twice had dialogues when she was in her nineties, wrote a novel at the age of one hundred. Perhaps I shall be as lucky as they in keeping my senses.

When I think back on my life, it is clear that luck, rather than any decision made after long deliberation, has governed my life. The accident of sitting next to a Chinese in an undergraduate class awakened an interest in his country and later in all of East Asia, which has grown with the years until it is now the most important part of my life. The outbreak of the Pacific War, just at a time when I had begun to study Japanese, determined my whole life.

A love of European classical music has been a part of me even longer than my love for Japan. This also was an accident. As a boy, music meant little to me. I took piano lessons from the age of seven, but they gave me no pleasure because I was aware of my clumsiness and I lacked the education in music that would have provided goals to attain if I practiced diligently. When I told my father I didn't enjoy practicing, he said I needn't go on with my piano lessons. I was delighted to be freed from the tedium of plodding through dreary pieces of music, but I have often wished that my father had spanked me and insisted that I continue my lessons. What pleasure it would give me now to be able to play the piano for my own enjoyment!

I remained ignorant of classical music until I was in high school, when a friend urged me to listen every Saturday night to the radio broadcasts of Toscanini conducting the NBC Symphony Orchestra. If I had not had this friend, would I have discovered classical music unaided?

The love of music exists independently of my love for Japan. I must confess that just as I do not like every variety of music, I do not appreciate equally every facet of Japanese culture. Although I have sometimes enjoyed classical Japanese music, it does not move me in the way that a Beethoven quartet, a song cycle by Schubert, or an opera by Verdi always does. Some may take this as proof that despite my devotion to Japanese culture, I am still a foreigner; but surely many Japanese share similar musical preferences.

If I have one complaint about my life in Japan, it is that many people, including some who have read my books, cannot believe that I read Japanese. When I am introduced after a lecture delivered in Japanese, some express apologies for not having a calling card in English or add *katakana* to help me read their names. A professor at Tokyo University commented about my history of Japanese, "I suppose you read in translation the works you discuss."

I also remain something of an outsider when it comes to food. I enjoy a bowl of miso soup once in a while, but I do not desire to have it every morning for breakfast. However, I never get tired of having a croissant and coffee for breakfast. What, I wonder,

has determined these tastes? Certainly not a yearning for food I ate as a child. As for coffee, I so disliked it that I never drank it while in college or during the war, though it was the only beverage the navy provided. Not until I was living in England and people made coffee especially for me, supposing that (as an

American) I would prefer it to tea, did I first drink coffee, in order not to disappoint my hosts. Now I feel as if it has always been an indispensable start to each day.

Tastes change, and it is conceivable that I may discover one day that I would like to have miso soup every morning. At present, however, when friends urge me to make preparations for old age by finding a suitable retirement home in Japan, the thought of a Japanese breakfast every day is a factor that keeps me from investigating such places. During the war I was convinced I was destined to survive unscathed, and today I have not yet accepted the fact that one day I may be unable to take care of myself and that I shall die. This foolish confidence, even more than miso soup, keeps me out of a retirement home.

I may well regret my inability to make preparations for my waning years, but looking back, I realize that things have generally turned out well, regardless of my actions. I seldom have had cause to regret anything. One of the few crucial decisions I made was to leave Cambridge for Columbia. At the time I feared I would regret leaving Cambridge. Indeed, whenever I have visited since then, I have been struck afresh by its beauty and wondered why I left. But without a second year of study in Japan (which Cambridge University refused me), I would not have made friendships that proved to be more precious than even the most beautiful surroundings.

I think, too, of the major changes in my life that never occurred. Had the civil war not broken out in 1936, I might have spent my life in Spain. If the "liberation" had not taken place in China in 1948, I might have become a scholar of Chinese literature. These possibilities (and there are others) are intriguing, but the conclusion is always the same: I was fantastically lucky. Greek tragedies often end with the warning that one should call no man happy until he is dead, and this may apply to me too, but at present my pervading emotion is one of gratitude, to my friends in different places and, above all, to Japan.

42

When I finished writing the last installment of my serial, I had a brief attack of the depression that in my case is likely to follow the accomplishment of any major task. Although this chronicle has continued for a full year, it was not on the scale of my history of Japanese literature, which took me twenty-five years to write, and the depression was proportionately smaller.

All the same, now that it was over, I felt pangs of regret. I failed to mention some experiences that might have been of particular interest to readers. I regretted even more that I had not mentioned many people who have played an important part in my life and should have appeared in my autobiography. They may wonder whether I thought less of them than of the persons about whom I have written, and if they have passed away, their families may wonder the same. I can only answer that once I began writing the chronicle, I became aware that I was describing something like a chain of linking experiences and that some friends, no matter how close, belonged to a different chain. It would not have been difficult to write an autobiography with a different cast of characters.

The most important of the "chains" in my life has been the one that binds me to Japan. For some years, especially when anti-Americanism was at its height in Japan, I worried that something might break the chain, that I would not be able to return. Fortunately, this did not happen. On the contrary, regardless of the plethora of anti-American writings, I have always been treated with great kindness, and not only by friends. Nowhere else would I have been given the opportunity to relate the events of my life in a newspaper that is read in every part of the country.

At first, when I began to write the chronicle, I planned to use, as examples of the changes that have occurred in my lifetime, the different modes of transport. This worked for a time. I recalled, for example, that when I was a boy, milk was delivered by the drivers of wagons pulled by horses. Such milk wagons probably no longer exist, but even more vivid in my memory is the clink of bottles of milk as they were set down every morning at the door by the driver. In the "mansion" where I live in Tokyo, there is a little cupboard for milk bottles built into the wall outside the door, proof that as recently as thirty-five years ago (when the building was erected) it was normal for milk to be delivered in bottles.

I often tell myself that I have basically not changed over the years but that the world has certainly changed, whether in small matters such as milk delivery or in the way of life of a whole nation. Could I have guessed when I was a child that a day would come when steam locomotives would be objects of nostalgia to people for whom airplanes had become the normal means of travel? In the future, airplanes and automobiles may seem quaint and nostalgic making to travelers who are accustomed to propel themselves through space in individual rockets.

Some things, probably the most important, remain the same. We feel this, for example, in reading *The Tale of Genji*. However greatly our lives differ from those of the aristocrats of a thousand years ago, the novel is fully intelligible because the emotions Murasaki Shikibu described are our own. Love, hatred, loneliness, jealousy, and the rest remain constant, regardless of changes in the mode of living. One of the great pleasures in reading the literature of the past, whether *The Tale of Genji* or Shakespeare, is to discover a communality of emotions, across time and space.

Some readers of my serial have expressed admiration for my ability to remember so much that happened long ago. I, on the contrary, am more aware of what I have forgotten. Recently I had the occasion to take out some old photographs. They show me standing next to other persons, all of us smiling at the camera. I don't remember either the places or who the people were. I search for a clue, perhaps words written on a wall in a foreign language, anything that might reveal in which country the picture was taken. All that survives of these moments are some photographs without captions.

I have often regretted that I haven't kept a diary. A diary would surely help me recapture much of the past. But perhaps it is just as well to have forgotten so much. If I remembered everything, I would recall things that frightened me when I was a small child, teachers I disliked at school, friends who I thought had betrayed me, people I loved who did not love me. No, it is probably better not to try to remember. I hope that this chronicle, for all its deficiencies, has at least suggested how one human being spent an essentially happy life.

With my father (to my left), boarding a ship in
Bremen to return to New York, summer 1931.

As a freshman at Columbia University, 1938.

Interrogating a prisoner of war on Okinawa. This photograph appeared in the July 20, 1945, issue of *Stars and Stripes*.

With Arthur Waley, outside King's College, Cambridge, probably 1953.

With Mrs. Okumura, sitting on the veranda of "my" house in Kyoto, 1954.

Performing as Tarōkaja in *Chidori*, September 13, 1956.

At Bashō's tomb in Zeze, 1955.

With Nagai Michio in Karuizawa,
around 1960.

With Stephen Spender and Angus Wilson at the Shōren-in, Kyoto, 1957. We were attending the PEN Club Congress.

Gathering of the Hachinoki Group at the house of Yoshida Ken'ichi, 1955. *From left to right:* Ōoka Shōhei, Mishima Yukio, Yoshida, me, Yoshikawa Itsuji, Jinzai Kiyoshi, and Fukuda Tsuneari.

Three American scholars of Japan—Howard Hibbett, Edward Seidensticker, and me—at the house of Tanizaki Jun'ichirō in Yugawara, September 6, 1964. To the right is Shimanaka Hōji, Tanizaki's publisher and my close friend.

With Abe Kōbō and Takemitsu Tōru.

Backstage with Mishima Yukio and Akutagawa Hiroshi, who was appearing in Mishima's play *Black Lizard*, 1962.

With Shiba Ryōtarō and Nagai Michio in New York on the occasion of the celebration marking my retirement, 1992.

With Ariyoshi Sawako and Abe Kōbō at a year-end party in my Tokyo apartment, around 1980.

Before the Golden Hall of the Chūson-ji,
summer 2006.

Teaching a class at home when an injury
prevented me from going to the university,
spring 2007. Not every student attended.

JAPANESE MENTIONED IN THE TEXT

Abe Kōbō (1924–1993)   Major novelist and playwright.

Abe Machi (1925–1993)   Wife of Abe Kōbō and, in her own right, an important stage designer and illustrator.

Ariyoshi Sawako (1931–1984)   Popular novelist who often treated social problems, such as aging and industrial pollution.

Ashikaga Yoshimasa (1436–1490)   The eighth shogun of the Muromachi shogunate, known for both his incompetence as a shogun and his extraordinary influence on Japanese taste.

Bashō (1644–1694)   Greatest of the haiku poets, also known for his beautifully written travel diaries.

Benkei (d. 1189)   Legendary warrior-monk whose exploits inspired many literary works.

Chikamatsu Monzaemon (1653–1724)   Dramatist who wrote for both the kabuki and bunraku theaters and usually is considered to be Japan's greatest playwright.

Ennin (794–864)   Buddhist monk who studied in China and left a major diary recording his experiences.

Fukazawa Shichirō (1914–1987)   Author of short stories and novels based mainly on folk tales and other lore.

Hirabayashi Taiko (1905–1971)   Writer who is known especially for her descriptions of poverty-striken people's lives.

Hirata Atsutane (1776–1843)   Author of many essays that describe his Shintō convictions.

Ikkyū (1394–1481)   Buddhist monk whose unconventional life and writings have made him a popular favorite.

Ishikawa Jun (1899–1987)   Novelist and scholar of both French and premodern Japanese literature.

Itō Sei (1905–1969)   Novelist and translator of English literature who is known best for his translation of *Lady Chatterley's Lover.*

Kanaseki Hisao (1918–1996)   Scholar of American literature and translator of several of my books.

Kaneko Keizō (b. 1932)   Photographer who took the photos for my books on nō and bunraku.

Kawabata Yasunari (1899–1972)   Major novelist and winner in 1968 of the Nobel Prize in Literature.

Kawakami Tetsutarō (1902–1988)   Essayist and critic of Japanese and foreign literature.

Kikuchi Kan (1888–1948)   Popular novelist and playwright who founded the magazine *Bungei shunjō* in 1923. The Kikuchi Kan Prize was established in his honor in 1938 and is awarded to persons who have contributed significantly to Japanese culture.

Kinoshita Junji (b. 1914)   Playwright and author of *Yūzuru* (*Twilight Crane*), a play that enjoyed great popularity.

Kuwabara Takeo (1904–1988)   Scholar of French and Japanese social and cultural history.

Matsumoto Kōshirō VIII (1910–1982)   Leading kabuki actor who specialized in strong, masculine roles.

Miyata Masayuki (1926–1997)   Artist who excelled particularly in paper-cut artwork (*kirie*) and designer of two of my books.

Mori Shū (1917–1987)   Specialist in the plays of Chikamatsu with whom I consulted when doing my translations.

Nagai Kafū (1879–1959)   Splendid writer, known for his devotion to both the licensed quarter and French literature.

Nagai Michio (1923–2000)   Scholar of education and my closest friend in Japan.

Nakamura Hiroko (b. 1944)   The most popular Japanese pianist of recent years and the wife of Shōji Kaoru.

Natsume Sōseki (1867–1916)   Novelist greatly admired by the Japanese, who tend to think of him as their most important writer.

Nishida Shizuko (1905–1976)   Painter and daughter of the celebrated philosopher Nishida Kitarō (1870–1945).

Nogami Yaeko (1885–1985)   Woman novelist of notably progressive views.

Ōe Kenzaburō (b. 1935)   Major novelist and winner in 1994 of the Nobel Prize in Literature who is much admired for his committed stand on social and political issues.

Ono no Komachi (ninth century)   Poet who is known for her love poetry.

Ōoka Shōhei (1909–1988)   Novelist who is remembered especially for his accounts of his experiences as a soldier and prisoner in the Philippines.

Osaragi Jirō (1897–1973)   Novelist who wrote many works based on Japanese history as well as others treating modern life.

Saikaku (1642–1693) (also known by full name, Ihara Saikaku)   Novelist of the Genroku era who wrote humorous fiction, mainly about the lives of commoners.

Sakurama Michio (1897–1983)   Actor of the Konparu school with whom I studied the singing of the nō texts.

Sasaki Mosaku (1894–1966)   Editor of *Bungei shunjū* and a judge of the Kikuchi Kan Prize.

Sasaki Nobutsuna (1872–1963)   Scholar of traditional Japanese poetry and prose.

Shiba Ryōtarō (1923–1996)   Highly popular writer, mainly of works of historical fiction.

Shiga Naoya (1883–1971)   Novelist and essayist who is greatly admired for his clear but evocative prose.

Shigeyama Sennojō (b. 1923)   *Kyōgen* actor with whom I studied.

Shinkei (1406–1475)   Buddhist priest and master of *renga* (linked verse).

Shinoda Hajime (1927–1989)   Esteemed critic of literature.

Shōji Kaoru (b. 1937)   Novelist who is known especially for works describing high school students.

Shōtoku (prince, 574–622)   Major figure in Japanese cultural history.

Taira no Munemori (1147–1185)   Warrior of the Taira family who figures in works of history and drama.

Takechi Tetsuji (1912–1988)   Director who is known especially for his imaginative productions of kabuki and modern plays.

Takemoto Tsunadayū (1906–1969)   Chanter of puppet plays performed at the Bunraku Theater.

Tamai Kensuke (1918–1990)   Chief editor of the magazine *Bunraku*, in which I published my first writings in Japanese.

Tanizaki Jun'ichirō (1886–1965)   Often rated as the greatest Japanese novelist of the twentieth century.

Teshigahara Hiroshi (b. 1927)   Film director and later head of the Sōgetsu school of flower arrangement.

Tokuoka Takao (b. 1930)   Journalist, critic, and one of my friends.

Tsunoda Ryūsaku (1877–1964)   Scholar who spent much of his life teaching at Columbia University and who was one of my teachers.

Uno Chiyo (1897–1996)   Author of autobiographical works and of stories that evoke the Japanese past.

Watanabe Kazan (1793–1841)   Painter who excelled especially at portraiture and who also was known for his patriotic writings.

Yokoyama Masakatsu (1912–2002)   Businessman with artistic interests who became a friend in China and with whom I maintained contact until his death.

Yokoyama Taikan (1868–1958)   The most celebrated Japanese painter of the twentieth century.

Yoshida Ken'ichi (1912–1977)   Essayist and scholar of English literature.

Yoshikawa Kōjirō (1904–1980)   Celebrated scholar of Chinese literature.

9 780231 144414